COOKING WITH DR. DOG

FROM BARE BONES TO BONE APPETIT

*Time-tested, favorite recipes recommended by Dr. Dog,
dedicated sniffer and taster of culinary delights.
Collected, tested, and edited by Jerry Jones.
Illustrated by Dr. Dog's human, Eric DeWitt.*

**"I prescribe this book for the novice, the
harried, and the culinarily challenged."
Dr. Dog**

J Jones Publishing
Black Mountain, North Carolina

Cover Design: Eric DeWitt
Original Illustrations: Eric DeWitt
Cover Photograph: Eric DeWitt

ISBN: 0-9676972-0-4
Library of Congress Card Number: 99-091632

Printed in the United States of America by CSS Publishing Company

First Edition

Dedicated to Julia Child
Without the inspiration and nurturing of
"Mastering the Art of French Cooking,"
this book might never have happened.

TABLE OF CONTENTMENT

ACKNOWLEDGEMENTS

Many thanks to that group of chefs and writers who produce the wonderful recipes, books, and magazines that serve as inspiration for all of us who enjoy good food well done.

In the SELECTED READINGS section of this book, you will find listed many of the publications that have been of particular influence to me over the years. And to think that the little bits of each one sampled in this collection are but a tiny fraction of the entire body of work.

So many cookbooks, so little time...

the dr. dog story

IS THERE A DOCTOR IN THE HOUSE?

The first time I met Dr. Dog (back then he was simply known as "Woof."), I was hanging out at the World Famous Exotic Patio Oyster Bar on Anna Maria Island on Florida's West Coast, soaking up inspiration. Gazing at the calm, green water of the Gulf of Mexico, wishing I were out sailing again, bound for all the enchanting places beyond the horizon (except Houston), I noticed approaching from the north a dejected looking fellow on all fours, clad only in a nondescript bit of fur, ambling aimlessly toward the bar. Ignoring all the invitations from beach creatures to play Frisbee Fetch, he appeared quite alone with his thoughts. Having been in that same circumstance some years ago, I decided to approach the chap and hear his story or perhaps offer some succor for his troubles.

That afternoon was the beginning of a long and excellent relationship that has culminated in the publication of this book.

Dr. Dog's (Woof's) story goes something like this:

As a young pup, he was recruited into the elite Canine Corps of the Drug Enforcement Agency as a drug sniffing dog. In the beginning, his acute sense of smell and instant evaluation of various materials filled his superiors with high hopes for his career. Indeed, he was one talented hound.

However, his career soon took a peculiar turn. Woof, you see, had a penchant for sniffing out what *he* considered important, not necessarily just what the DEA was seeking. And what Woof thought important was food. Good food. Delectable tidbits. In fact, Woof had an infallible ability to detect the slightest trace of gourmet food items being brought into this country and aggressively pointed them out to the customs agents.

To this day, he doesn't understand why that cost him his job. As he told me, much of this stuff was being brought into the country quite illegally or without respect for proper payment of duty. His argument fell on deaf ears, however, and soon Woof found himself on the street, without so much as a bag of Kibbles and Bits.

We got along well on the beach that day, and I asked him if he might be interested in hanging out with me and my wife in our little beachfront home. "It's not much," I said, "but we've got a rug on the floor, a bowl of food, water, and plenty of flea powder. " I think the last won him over. In any case, Woof accepted my offer, and off we rode with the top down, his ears flapping in the breeze, a wide grin on his face.

I've always been something of an amateur chef and love preparing new and different foods. "Enjoy it this time," the saying goes around our house, "because he'll probably never get around to making it again." Woof became a willing participant in my culinary experimentation and before long, everything was put to the Woof "sniff and taste" test.

We still knew our new canine companion simply as Woof until one day a strange and serendipitous incident occurred. The phone rang, and a stressed-filled voice on the other end asked, "Is there a doctor available?"

"A doctor?" I answered.

"Yes," the voice replied. "Isn't this the number for Rx for Recipes?" Not waiting for my reply, the caller pressed on urgently. "I'm having a terrible problem with a recipe, you see, and I hoped one of your doctors could help."

"I see," I replied, not really seeing, but intrigued. And then in a moment of inspiration, seeing Woof outside with a lady friend in the front yard, I added, "Oh, perhaps you need the help of Dr. Dog."

"Dr. Dawk?"

"Uh, yes. Something like that. But I'm afraid he is rather tied up at the moment. Perhaps if you could relate your problem to me, I could be of some assistance."

"Oh, thank you, thank you!" she replied, relief surging through her voice, and then she launched into her problem about some now-forgotten difficulty with a recipe. I offered her some advice, suggested she take two shots of sherry and call me in the morning if things didn't work. I never heard from her again, but her call gave me an idea.

If Dr. Dog, as he was to be known henceforth, and I could work together to sniff out recipe problems, and discover new gastronomical delights, then perhaps someday we could collaborate on a comprehensive cookbook for the neophyte, the cook on the go, and the culinarily challenged.

And here it is. *Cooking with Dr. Dog*, with the assistance of myself and a most talented designer, Eric DeWitt, who is now Dr. Dog's personal human being.

Although created with tongue in cheek, this is a serious work. The recipes selected for this book are a collection of our favorites, compiled from other cookbooks, family, friends, newspapers, magazines, and my own (and Dr. Dog's) experimentation. Please refer to the bibliography at the back of the book for a list of *Selected Reading* wherein I have tried to give credit to the many wonderful chefs whose talent and skill in the kitchen have given untold hours of pleasure. Where I am aware of the origin or inspiration of the recipe I have given credit.

Jerry Jones

cooking with okrah

SO DR. DOG, WHY HAVE YOU DECIDED TO COLLABORATE ON A COOKBOOK?

WELL, IT ALL STARTED WHEN I WAS A PUPPY. MY MOM ABANDONED ME & I LOST MY JOB AND... HUH? OH SORRY, WRONG SHOW. ANYWAY...

OKRAH, TOO LONG THIS INDUSTRY HAS BEEN DOMINATED BY HEALTHY, FAT FREE COOK BOOKS...

YAY CLAP CLAP

WELL THERE YOU HAVE IT FOLKS, STRAIGHT FROM THE DOGS MOUTH, WHICH IS CLEANER THAN A HUMANS I HEAR IF I WAS A COOK, I'D BUY THIS BOOK! SEE YOU LATER!

starting from scratch

STARTING FROM SCRATCH

EQUIPMENT

There is a never ending array of kitchen gadgets and equipment. You don't need them all, so get what is useful to you at the moment and add the others as the need arises or the spirit moves you. The following list is in no particular order.

Skillets. I experimented with a variety of skillets a few years back, and the only conclusion I could reach was that an inexpensive, non-stick skillet of sufficiently thick aluminum was the only way to go. For about $12, you can buy a nice looking, heavy (or heavy enough) aluminum, non-stick, three skillet set. When the non-stick gets bad, throw them away and buy another set. I suggest you buy a large (12") skillet as well. You just can't fry a whole chicken in a 10" skillet. There are some great new skillets out now that are wide, deep, have glasses lids and will work as a wok, large saucepan, small dutch oven or about anything. In addition, a 10" cast iron skillet, properly seasoned, works about as well as non-stick and does things that a lighter skillet just won't do. For example: baking jalapeno cornbread, pan broiling a filet, or blackening fish.

Dutch Ovens. For soups and stews and the like, you need a four-quart and a six-quart Dutch oven. Here I favor a good quality stainless steel pot with a steel clad copper bottom. FARBERWARE® makes an excellent set that includes the Dutch ovens, sauce pans, a double boiler unit and a skillet for about $80. - a worthwhile investment that should last you forever (available in non-stick as well).

Sauce pans. You need one, two and three-quart sauce pans. See above for recommendations.

Spatulas. Stainless, plastic, wooden, flexible, slotted. You need a collection.

Garlic Press. An essential if you use garlic. It works for minced, pressed, just about any way the recipe indicates. The self-cleaning ones are nice.

Knives. A large French chef knife is essential. Learn to use it, and mincing and dicing will be a lot easier. In addition, a filet knife, paring knives and a couple of utility knives are helpful. To slice bread, you will need a serrated bread knife. A cleaver may be of use to you also, although probably not very often.

Tongs. Useful for picking up things firmly and for turning things in a skillet and on the grill without puncturing them. Spaghetti tongs will help you keep a grip on things, too.

Whisks. An assortment of various size balloon whisks are useful for making dressings and sauces, beating eggs, whipping cream and blending ingredients. A little coiled wire whisk is good for working in small quantities and in shallow containers.

Hand Held Electric Mixer. You can whip cream, beat egg whites and mix bread and cake ingredients by hand, but a mixer sure takes a lot of the work out of it. Get one with plenty of power.

Food Processor. This machine saves so much time and effort that it is tempting to call it a necessity. It is, if you are a serious and busy cook. As far as the machine itself goes, nothing really quite matches a CUISINART®, but some of the far less expensive ones get close enough to make it worthwhile.

Blender. A blender is great for making drinks, pureeing soups and making bread crumbs. My favorite use is to make sauces like Hollandaise and Bearnaise. Easy and foolproof.

Mallet. Occasionally you need something to flatten something else with, such as a chicken breast or a piece of meat. If you don't have an official mallet, a rolling pin or heavy bottle will suffice.

Knife Sharpener. There are a variety to choose from. Pick one and learn to use it. Nothing is as inadequate as a dull knife. Have your knives sharpened professionally once in a while.

Kitchen Utensil Set. A " set" consists of at least a soup ladle, a large spoon, a large slotted spoon and a long-tined fork. Mix or match to get what satisfies you.

Wooden Spoons. Nothing beats wooden spoons for stirring. Keep several.

Timer. Even though you may have a stove timer and a timer on the microwave, a third one will come in handy more often than you can believe.

Glass Measuring Cups. You need at least one two- cup glass measuring cup. Glass goes everywhere: stovetop, oven, microwave, freezer. If you are inclined to cook with a microwave, larger capacity ones are very useful.

Measuring Cups and Spoons. For general measuring, I prefer metal cups and spoons. They are more durable, easier to clean and don't melt if you leave them too near something hot.

Sifter. If you bake at all, you will need a sifter. A two-cup sifter will be adequate. If you want to avoid sifting, use one of the instant blending flours such as *Gold Medal's Wondra®* or *Pillsbury's Shake & Blend®*. They are great for lump-free sauces, gravies and rouxes. When measuring, sift the flour first into the measuring cup, then level the top with the edge of a knife.

Hot Pads. Keep several around and avoid burned fingers.

Cookie Sheets and Pizza Pans. These are handy for a lot more things than pizza and cookies. They are good for heating up things, baking potatoes, and serving as a drip pan under something else.

Muffin Tins. If you want to make muffins, you will be hard pressed to find another way. The mini-muffin tins are fun, too.

Grater. The four-sided metal grater hasn't seen a technological revolution since its invention a century and a half ago. If you are doing great volumes, crank up the food processor, but for most applications, this is all you need. It works for vegetables, cheeses and whole nutmeg. (You'll never use pre-ground again.) The only thing that baffles me is how do you *really* grate ginger. The cookbooks breeze right by it with no note that you really can't do this and that anything approximating a fibrous mass will be just fine.

Wok. If you develop an interest in Oriental cooking and stir frying, get a wok, a BIG wok. And hopefully, a gas stove.

Vertical Roaster. A vertical roaster is a device upon which you mount a chicken through the body cavity and the neck hole. A really excellent and simple way to prepare roast chicken. You can carve it right off the stand.

Vegetable Peeler. A must-have for removing the skin from potatoes and vegetables. There are two types: one is grasped like a knife and pushed or pulled and one that is grasped by the end and pulled across the vegetable. I prefer the latter type.

Microwave. I could live without a microwave easily. I rarely do frozen microwave dinners and prefer them cooked in the oven anyway. There are some good microwave cookbooks, but though I have tried, I just can't make a commitment to it. Microwaves are great for melting butter and for warming coffee and leftovers. They will boil a quart of water in only slightly more time than you can do it on the range top. Doing rice and spaghetti is nonsense. They will do a quick "baked" potato and a very nice baked onion (wrapped in plastic wrap with some butter and nutmeg), but all in all, the thing I use most on a microwave is the timer.

Casseroles and Other Baking Utensils. One, two and three-quart Corning Ware® casseroles are useful for a number of things. You will also find a Pyrex® 9 X 2 X 13 pan often comes in handy, as well as a metal or glass loaf pan or two. You may also want a pie plate and a cake pan. These are the kinds of things that can wait until you need them.

Dinnerware and Serving Pieces. Pretty plates and flatware, and attractive serving dishes make a pleasant table. If you want something besides your everyday stuff, buy a few nice pieces. Get only a service for four. Or mix things up. Use nice placemats and napkins and get some inexpensive, but matching goblets and wine glasses. Instead of using a lot of serving pieces that you don't have and would have to wash anyway, serve restaurant style. Arrange the food on the plates in the kitchen and bring it to the dining area. This gives you the opportunity to make things pretty and saves your guest the uneasiness and hassle of serving him/herself. Besides, all those serving dishes really clutter up a table that is much more attractive with candles and flowers. Don't forget the music.

Candles and Candlesticks. Get some long tapers and some nice candle holders. They are romantic and if you have screwed something up a little bit, maybe she won't notice. That's how I used to slip medium rare tenderloin, which I couldn't bear to overcook, past people who thought they could only eat it well-done. Always burn your candle a little before your guests come. They'll think you dine by candlelight all the time.

Ziploc® Bags. Pints, quarts, and gallons. Get the freezer types for durability. They are great not only for storage, but ideal for marinating meats and transporting prepared foods to the site of consumption. For example, put the chili in a bag, put in the ice chest, and when it's time, put it in a pot to heat it. Saves a lot of space, clean-up and mess.

Miscellaneous items.
> Crockpot
> Candy thermometer
> "Instant read" meat thermometer
> Warming trays
> Colanders (2)
> Salad spinner (to wash and dry lettuce and greens)
> Aluminum foil
> Wax paper
> Plastic wrap
> Mixing bowls (a stainless set at least)
> Can opener (non-electric)
> Cutting board
> Propane BBQ pit
> Chafing dish
> Pizza stone and baker's peel

There are lots of other things, but you'll discover those as you get more adventurous.

INGREDIENTS

Ingredients basically break down into staples (items that have a long shelf life and should be on hand for day-to-day use), and perishables. The perishables also break down into those with a very short use period and those that may last a while longer, either naturally or extended by refrigeration or freezing.

STAPLES

The following list is basically what I keep on hand (plus a lot more that has accumulated) and use fairly regularly. Do not rush out and buy all this stuff until your menu for the week includes a recipe that requires it. There is no point in investing in inventory that may not be used for months, if ever.

Flour. A five pound bag of all purpose flour (not self-rising) and a small bag or shaker carton of an instant blending flour will last a considerable time unless you start baking a lot.

Baking Powder. Needed when baking.

Baking Soda. Likewise.

Sugar. A five pound bag of sugar lasts me a very long time. Unless you foresee using a lot, you may want to invest in a two pound bag instead.

Brown Sugar. I keep a small bag on hand.

Olive Oil. A healthy cooking oil and my favorite. There are a number of grades of olive oil, depending on the pressing and other factors. The price varies accordingly. My favorite inexpensive oil is *Bertolli Extra Virgin®* , and it has a pale green cast to it. I usually buy it in a large bottle at *Sam's Club®*. When the budget allows, try some of more exotic brands from small producers. There are some remarkable taste differences. Olive oil is wonderful brushed on bread as a substitute for mayonnaise.

Canola Oil. Where olive oil is not appropriate, I use canola oil. Canola oil, a derivative of the rapeseed, is considered a "healthy" oil.

Salt. Salt is salt, although I like using Kosher salt because of the large, granular texture.

Instant Mashed Potatoes. While I am not normally disposed towards convenience foods, instant mashies really are a time saver and some of them don't taste too bad. I like *Potato Buds®*. Don't try to make potato pancakes, though, they just won't work. Potato soup? Yes.

Tuna Fish. A reliable stand-by in case of hunger attacks.

Vinegar. I keep several kinds - plain white, apple cider, red wine, tarragon, and the wonderful Balsamic. There are lots of others that come and go in popularity.

Jiffy® Mixes. Jiffy makes cornbread and muffin mixes that are so inexpensive and easy (and good) that there should always be a few on the shelf in case a craving strikes at 11:00 PM.

Pastas. Pastas are good comfort foods and easy to figure out something to do with. I usually have fettucini and linguini around. Fettucini Alfredo is easy to do, as is linguini with clam sauce. Keep a can or two of *Progresso®* clam sauce (white or red or both) and when you are out of money, time or ideas, you will have a fallback. Orzo is a rice-shaped pasta that is a great replacement when you tire of rice.

Miscellaneous.

Catsup	Soy sauce
Mayonnaise	Bottled lemon juice
Prepared mustard	Olives
Dijon Mustard	Tabasco
Worchestershire sauce	Tomato sauce
Hershey's Cocoa	Colman's Mustard (dry)

Spices. I maintain a very large array of spices because I do a lot of different cuisines. Here again, check your recipes to see what is called for. As you become more familiar with them, experiment. What basil or thyme or many other spices can do for plain boiled green beans is almost magic. Some natural foods stores sell fresh spices in bulk for far less cost than the outrageous prices found on packaged spices in the grocery store. For example, a typical bottle of oregano bought at the grocery contains .43 ounces of oregano. It costs $1.89. At my local natural foods store, I pay $.17.

PERISHABLES

Meats and Poultry. Buy fresh as needed, except when you can get really good deals that make freezing worthwhile. Whole fryers at a good price is an example. Pre-frozen boneless, skinless chicken breasts and thighs are a great convenience. You can get these by the bag at most grocery stores for a reasonable price.

Some grocery stores mark down meat if it is a day old. It has probably lost its red, fresh-cut color, but there is absolutely nothing wrong with it and the price cut is usually dramatic.

Seafood. Always buy seafood as near to the time you plan to use it as you can. Make sure it looks fresh and smells fresh.

Vegetables. Always buy fresh if you can and if you can find a local produce stand or farmer's market, you will be a lot better off cost-wise and quality-wise. The grocery chains don't seem aware that vegetables are grown locally almost everywhere and instead ship them indiscriminately from one coast to the other. But when dealing with "polyethylene" tomatoes, I guess a little shipping can't do much harm. For the best buys, try to use what is in season. If you must have a vegetable that is not in season or not available fresh, go next to frozen. For example, green peas and lima beans are almost never available fresh and frozen spinach is the only way spinach makes sense, except for salads. Buy the chopped, though, not the leaf. Canned vegetables have their uses, but not too often as stand alone items. Canned pinto, kidney and black beans are fine, especially when you are in a hurry. Canned artichokes, new potatoes, corn, and mushrooms are useful. All the variations on canned tomatoes (pureed, crushed, whole, stewed, etc.) are not only useful, but in much cooking, critical.

Fruits. Buy fresh fruits for most of your needs. However, canned pineapple, pears and mandarin oranges may be useful. Frozen fruits have occasional uses, but they tend to assume a Frosty the Snowman posture when thawed.

Coffee. Having owned a coffee shop, I guess I am spoiled to the taste of specialty coffees, to the point I will rarely subject myself to those sold in supermarkets. The key to a good coffee is freshness--the fresher the bean, the fresher the roast, the fresher the brew, the better the coffee. If you can afford it, buy whole coffee beans in bulk from a reliable specialty coffee store and grind your own. Always store coffee, no matter where you've purchased it, in a Freezer Ziploc®.

Tea. The same holds true in general for tea, although supermarkets do carry some good teas. Ziploc® freezer storage is also recommended, even for tea bags.

Canned Evaporated Milk. A great emergency substitute when you run out of milk. It will also serve as a cream substitute and will even whip.

Canned Soups. Called for in many recipes and also a handy emergency meal. Try tomato soup with some basil and a touch of butter and sherry.

BASIC INSTRUCTIONS

This chapter is devoted to some of the more basic activities involved in cooking: how to cook eggs, how to peel certain vegetables and other time saving tricks to take the mystery and uncertainty out of your efforts.

Eggs. There are four basic ways that eggs are commonly cooked: they are boiled, poached, fried or scrambled.

To boil an egg is simple, but to boil an egg and get perfect results (no green ring around the yolk, for example) takes a little more effort. Start by piercing the large end of the egg with a needle or other sharp object. (I keep a map tack stuck in the side of my utensil drawer for this purpose.) This lets the air out and prevents the egg shell from cracking. Place the eggs in a pot of cold water. Bring the water to a boil, remove from heat, cover and let stand 17 minutes. Pour off water and cool with cold water. After the eggs have cooled, shake them around in the pan to crack and loosen the shells. Peel. There are a couple of other steps that some people advise, but this is sufficient.

To fry an egg and make it look good takes low heat and patience. Heat an eighth inch of so of oil in a skillet. When hot, gently slide the egg (from a saucer) into the skillet. When the white begins to set, spoon or splash the hot oil over the egg to cook the top. This is known as "sunny side up". To make it "over", flip it over. Cook to desired doneness.

To poach an egg properly requires a really fresh farmyard egg. Alas, those are hard to come by. The problem is that runny eggs tend to diffuse through the cooking water rather than coagulating properly. Start with a wide, non-stick skillet. Heat a couple of inches of water until tiny bubbles start to rise. Maintain that condition. Add a tablespoon of vinegar to the water. (This helps the coagulation.)

Very, very carefully slide the egg from a saucer or large spoon into the water. Disturb as little as possible until set. Add the other eggs very carefully. When they set, they will tend to rise toward the top. You made need to gently loosen them from the bottom of the skillet (even a non-stick). When they are done to your satisfaction, remove them to a bowl of hot water until you have finished poaching. Remove with a slotted spoon.

To scramble eggs properly takes low heat and patience as well. If you are going to do half a dozen eggs, melt a quarter stick of butter in a skillet over low heat. When the butter is melted, break the eggs into the skillet. Let them cook until the whites are pretty well set, then start to move the yolks about.

At some point you have to make the decision to start breaking the yolks. The appearance of the finished eggs and the curd size will depend on that It is subject to experimentation. Just before the eggs are done, (be careful not to overcook) add another quarter stick of butter, melt slightly and remove from heat to finish melting. Add salt and pepper, sour cream if you like, and you should have creamy, moist scrambled eggs.

Bacon. This is where the microwave shines. Line a plate with paper towels, lay out the bacon and cover with paper towels. Microwave on high for about one minute per slice. To cook conventionally, cook VERY slowly. Newly available is pre-cooked bacon that requires no refrigeration until the package is opened. A great convenience, you don't have to deal with the grease and it costs about the same as raw bacon.

Garlic. To make peeling garlic easy, lay the clove on a flat surface, (a cutting board is a good choice), and press the flat side of a knife firmly against it. The skin should then pull right off. Incidentally, to remove the garlic smell from your hands, run cold water over your hands or fingers while rubbing the affected area with the blade of a stainless steel knife (or a stainless thing anything, I suppose). I have no explanation for why this works, but it does.

Onions. Many recipes call for diced onions. I searched for years for a new technique for this procedure, but still haven't discovered one. However, there is a little trick that helps. Trim the onion, but do not cut off the root end. Slice the onion vertically down to the root end, rotate ninety degrees and cut the other way. Then, when you slice off your dice the onion will hold together much better. To peel small onions, boil them for about 15-20 seconds and the skins should slip off.

Tomatoes. To peel a tomato the easy way, just dip it in boiling water for 15 seconds. The peel slides right off.

The Hollandaise Sauce Family. The Hollandaise sauce "family" consists of hollandaise, bearnaise, maltaise, choron, sabayon, etc., all variations a on a delicious theme.

Bearnaise is made with wine, vinegar, shallots and tarragon instead of the lemon juice of hollandaise.

Maltaise is orange flavored Hollandaise.

Choron is tomato flavored bearnaise.

Sabayon is Hollandaise with cream and a white wine fish stock.

You can make up your own. See the PUP-POURRI section for easy instructions on how to make blender Hollandaise..

Gravy. I hesitate to give advice on this because I have always done it by "feel". If I were to fry a chicken and wished to make gravy, this is what I would do:

Pour some of the oil out the pan so that there is probably a table-spoon or two left. Over medium heat, sprinkle in what I judge to be about enough flour to absorb the oil (use instant blending to assure lump-free results) and brown the flour, stirring all the while, until quite dark. Then I would add water, probably a couple of cups, or milk, or a mixture. It will thicken rapidly. If necessary add more liquid, stirring constantly. When thickened to my satisfaction, I would taste for salt, adjust if necessary, and remove from the heat. A little experience will teach you your own way.

Roux. A sort of gravy used as a base for soups and, notably, gumbo. Flour is cooked very slowly in oil to the point that it almost burns, and then other things are added. This used to be a forty five or fifty minute job to which constant attention had to be paid. The microwave makes it easy. Watch for instructions in the PUP-POURRI section.

dr. dog's 1st lesson
don't lick the ice cube tray!

first licks

FIRST LICKS

APPETIZERS

ANTIPASTO ON A STICK

1/3 C. olive oil
1/4 C. apple cider vinegar
1/2 C. beer
1/2 tsp. salt
1/2 tsp. sugar
1/2 tsp. dry mustard
1/2 tsp. oregano
1/2 tsp. black pepper
8 oz. package mozzarella cheese
8 oz. sliced salami
24 cherry tomatoes
12 small mushrooms, trimmed
6 oz. jar of marinated artichoke hearts (divided into 12 pieces)
24 pitted ripe olives

Combine olive oil, vinegar, beer, salt, sugar, oregano and ground pepper in jar with a lid. Mix well.

Cut mozzarella into 3 thick slices, then cut each slice into 6 sticks. Wrap each stick inside a slice of salami, cut in half crosswise, fasten each half with a toothpick.

Thread 2 tomatoes, 1 mushroom, 1 piece of artichoke heart, 3 salami rolls, and 2 olives onto each of 12 skewers, place in shallow baking dish. Drizzle dressing over top. Allow antipasto to marinate 2 or more hours so flavors will blend.

At serving time, drain and arrange on tray.

BULGOGGI (A Korean barbecue beef appetizer)

1 lb. London broil or other beef roast cut into pieces 1-1/2 to 2 inches thick
2 Tbs. Oriental (dark) sesame oil
1/4 C. soy sauce
1 tsp. garlic powder
1 1/2 tsp. vinegar
Pepper
1 1/2 tsp. crushed toasted sesame seeds*
1/4 tsp. cayenne (more or less, as desired)
1 green onion and top, thinly sliced

Cut meat across grain into very thin slices (easier if you partially freeze the meat first). If slices are longer than 3 inches, cut them in half. Place meat in a bowl with oil, soy sauce, garlic powder, vinegar, a sprinkling of pepper, the crushed sesame seeds, cayenne and onion. Mix with your hands until well blended. Cover and refrigerate for at least four hours.

To cook, place meat over a very hot charcoal fire or gas grill (you will need some sort of screen to prevent the meat from falling through the grill) and cook a minute or so on each side.
NOTE: No matter how few people or how much meat, there is never enough of this compelling morsel, so I suggest you start out by at least doubling the recipe.

* **Crushed toasted sesame seeds.** Place sesame seeds in a heavy frying pan. Stirring, cook over medium heat for about ten minutes or until golden brown. Turn seed into a mortar or blender, add one teaspoon salt for each cup of seed and crush with a pestle or blend. Store in a tightly covered jar.

CHERRY TOMATOES WITH SMOKED OYSTERS

Cherry tomatoes
Canned smoked oysters

Slice the top off the tomatoes and remove seeds and pulp with small spoon or melon baller. Stuff with one oyster per tomato.

PARMESAN PUFFS

¹/₄ C. milk
¹/₄ C. water
¹/₂ stick unsalted butter
¹/₄ tsp. salt
¹/₂ C. all-purpose flour
2 large eggs
1 C. Parmesan cheese
Ground black pepper

In a small heavy saucepan, combine milk, water, butter and salt and bring the mixture to a boil over high heat. Reduce the heat to moderate, add the flour all at once and beat the mixture with a wooden spoon until it leaves the side of the pan and forms a ball.

Transfer mixture to a bowl, whisk in the eggs, one at a time, whisking well after each addition, and stir in the Parmesan and pepper to taste.

Drop the batter in small mounds on a buttered baking sheet and bake the puffs in the upper third of a preheated 400° F. oven for 20 minutes or until they are crisp and golden.

The puffs may be served as an hors d'ouevre or as an accompaniment to soups, meat or poultry. They are best served immediately, but may be stored overnight in an airtight container. Makes 20-24.

ROSELYN'S ARTICHOKE SPREAD

1 C. mayonnaise
1 C. fresh grated parmesan
2 Tbs. sour cream
1 large can artichokes
Chopped mushrooms (optional)

Mix all ingredients together and bake in a 400° F. oven for 10 minutes. Serve with crackers or thin bread rounds. If available, try this with rosemary olive bread--sensational!

WHOLE BAKED GARLIC WITH TOASTS

1 large head of garlic
3 Tbs. olive oil
1/4 inch thick diagonal baguette slices

Cut off the top 1/4 of the garlic with a sharp knife to expose the cloves, set the garlic in the middle of a large piece of foil, and drizzle it with 2 tsp. of the oil. Crimp the foil around the garlic to enclose it completely and bake the garlic in the middle of a preheated 425° F. oven for 40 minutes.

While the garlic is baking, brush the bread slices with the remaining oil and bake them on a baking sheet in the lower third of the oven (below the garlic), turning them once, for 10 to 12 minutes, or until they are golden and crisp. Unwrap the garlic and put it on a serving plate surrounded by the toasts.

To serve the garlic, remove the softened cloves with a knife or fork, or turn the head of garlic upside down and squeeze out the cloves, and spread the garlic on the toasts. Serves 2 as a first course.

BRUSCHETTA AL POMODORO

8 small slices of Italian or other coarse textured bread cut 1/2 inch thick
1 clove garlic, cut in half
salt and pepper
Olive oil
2 large, ripe tomatoes, roughly chopped
1 small sweet onion, chopped
4 anchovy fillets (optional)

Toast the bread on both sides. Rub one side with cut garlic. Sprinkle with salt and pepper and olive oil. Cover the toast with tomatoes, top with a sprinkling of onion and the optional 1/2 anchovy fillet.

For a variations on this theme, spread toast with cream cheese, top with a slice of smoked salmon, and sprinkle with fresh dill.

BAKED BRIE

4 oz. round of Brie cheese
1 garlic clove, minced
2 Tbs. butter, melted
Toasted slivered almonds

Mix minced garlic with melted butter and almonds. Place Brie on microwave-safe dish. Pour butter mixture over Brie. Microwave on high 20-30 seconds. Serve warm with fresh fruit and toasted slices of French bread or bagels.

CHUTNEY AND CREAM CHEESE

8 oz. block of cream cheese
Jar of chutney, such as Major Grey's®

Pour chutney over room temperature cream cheese. Serve with crackers. Or try PICKAPEPPA® sauce instead of chutney. Strawberry preserves work well , too. Sweet jalapenos give it a surprising zip.

SALMON CHEESEBALL

1 large (7 ¾ oz.) can red salmon, drained and flaked
8 oz. cream cheese, softened
1 Tb. lemon juice
1 Tb. grated onion
1 tsp. prepared horseradish
¼ tsp. liquid smoke
Chopped parsley

Combine all ingredients except parsley. Chill. Shape into 4-inch ball and roll in parsley. Serve with crackers. Makes about 2 cups.

SHRIMP MOUSSE

1 can condensed tomato soup
1 envelope unflavored gelatin
1/3 C. water
2 3 oz. packages of cream cheese
1 C. mayonnaise
1/2 C. celery, minced
1/2 C. sliced green onions, more if desired
1/4 tsp. basil
2 5 oz. cans shrimp

Drain shrimp and place in a bowl of lemon juice or vinegar and ice water with ice for 15 minutes, drain.

Heat the soup. While it is heating, put the gelatin in 1/3 cup of water to soften, then pour into soup. Add the softened cream cheese to soup and blend with rotary beater or spoon. Remove from heat, add mayonnaise, celery, onions, basil and shrimp. Pour into four cup mold. Refrigerate until set.

Unmold and serve with crackers as a dip, or with a small knife.

TACO SALAD DIP

1 large can bean dip
3 avocados, chopped
3 Tbs. lemon juice
8 oz. sour cream
1/2 C. mayonnaise
1 pkg. taco seasoning
1 C. or more chopped green onions
2 C. chopped tomatoes
1 1/2 C. shredded sharp Cheddar cheese
1 C. chopped black olives

Spread bean dip on a large platter. Mash avocados with lemon juice and spread over bean dip. Blend sour cream, mayonnaise and taco seasoning and spread over avocados. Sprinkle tomatoes and green onions over sour cream mixture. Top with Cheddar cheese and garnish with ripe olives. Serve with tortilla or corn chips.

AUNT NORINE'S ASPARAGUS ROLLS

1 loaf Pepperidge Farm thin sliced white bread
2 sticks butter
1 pkg. frozen asparagus spears
8 oz. cream cheese
4 oz. crumbled bleu cheese
Garlic powder to taste

Cut crusts from bread slices and flatten slices with a rolling pin. Melt the butter in a saucepan. Mix together cream cheese, bleu cheese and garlic powder. Spread mix on unbuttered slices of bread. Roll each asparagus spear in a slice of bread. Dip roll in butter. Lay separately on foil and freeze. When ready to use, cut each bread roll into 3 pieces. Bake for 10 minutes at 350° F.

BEVERAGES

SPARKLING SCREWDRIVERS

6 oz. can frozen orange juice
1 C. vodka
32 oz. club soda or seltzer
Mint for garnish

Mix frozen concentrate with vodka. Add soda. Stir until orange juice melts and blends with other liquids. Pour over ice and garnish with mint.

BASIC BLOODY MARY

1 large can tomato juice
2 Tbs. prepared horseradish
2 Tbs. Worchestershire sauce
Juice of 1/2 of a lime
Tabasco, salt and pepper to taste
Lime wedges to garnish
Vodka to taste (a cup or so).

Mix all ingredients in a large pitcher and serve in cocktail glasses over ice. Garnish with lime. Serves 4-6.

THE CLASSIC MARTINI

1½ oz. good gin or vodka
¼ tsp. vermouth
Olives or twists of lemon rind

Preferences vary on how to mix a martini. "Stirred, not shaken," says James Bond. Others like chilling with a shaker. If using a shaker, fill it first with ice. Then drizzle the vermouth over the ice, then add gin or vodka. The less vermouth, the "drier" the martini. Shake and strain into martini glasses. Garnish with olives or lemon twist.

MOTHER'S COURAGE

An old recipe from the Roux family of Savannah, this concoction was first served to mother to give her courage when sailing. It later became an antidote for the "arsenic hour" (suppertime with small children). It has also proved to be effective when dealing with teenagers. Roux brides are given a special crystal container to store her courage in the freezer. Make this ahead and freeze for occasions calling for extra courage!

3 jiggers gin
3 jiggers vodka
1 jigger vermouth
2 drops of Scotch (this takes the curse off)

ix together the above ingredients, decant and put into the freezer. When ready to serve, use a silver spoon to crush ice wrapped in a linen tea towel. Serve the Courage over crushed ice in an old fashion cocktail glass. Add a twist of lemon and two olives.

THE ORIGINAL PINA COLADA

1 C. pineapple juice
1/2 C. cream of coconut
4 jiggers rum
4 C. ice

In blender, combine all ingredients and blend on high 20-30 seconds. Serve immediately. Garnish with fresh pineapple or Maraschino cherries. Serves 4.

PERFECT MARGARITAS

1/2 C. freshly squeezed lime juice, flesh and all
1/2 C. triple sec
11/2 C. tequila
Coarse salt (Kosher salt is great for this)
Ice

Prepare glasses in advance by rubbing the rims with lime rind and pressing into salt in a small saucer. Place glasses in freezer.
     Combine lime juice, triple sec and tequila in a cocktail shaker, add ice, and shake vigorously. Strain into the prepared glasses and garnish with a thin slice of lime. Makes 4 large margaritas.
     NOTE: For the best margaritas, buy the 92 proof variety made from 100% blue agave, also known as mescal.

MANGO DAIQUIRI

4 oz. rum
1 oz. Triple Sec (a little more if the mangoes are not real sweet)
1/2 of a chopped mango
2 Tbs. lime juice
1 Tb. sugar
2 C. crushed ice

B lend all together and serve. This is guaranteed to cool you off on a hot day. Works great with peaches, too.

SEA BREEZE

1 1/2 - 2 oz. vodka
1/4 C. chilled grapefruit juice
1/4 C. chilled cranberry juice
1 small grapefruit wedge for garnish

M ix the vodka, grapefruit and cranberry juices, pour over ice. Garnish with grapefruit wedge. Serves 1.

PLANTER'S PUNCH

2/3 C. dark rum
1/4 C. fresh lime juice
1/4 C. triple sec
1 Tb. grenadine
1/2 tsp. Angostura bitters
1/2 C. fresh orange juice
4 bamboo skewers, each threaded with a lime wedge, orange wedge, and a Maraschino cherry

C ombine all liquids in a cocktail shaker half filled with ice. Shake for 30 seconds, strain into 4 tall glasses filled with ice. Garnish with skewered fruit and lime slices. Serves 4.

JAMAICA FAREWELL

Cracked ice
1 C. fresh orange juice
3/4 C. tequila
1/2 C. Tia Maria
3-4 Tbs. fresh lime juice
4 orange slices

Fill cocktail shaker with cracked ice. Add all ingredients except orange slices. Shake until frosted. Strain into tall glasses filled with cracked ice. Garnish with orange. Serves 4.

GOOMBAY SMASH

10 oz. fresh orange juice
10 oz. pineapple juice
5 oz. dark rum
4 oz. coconut rum
2 oz. Bacardi 151
1 1/2 oz. apricot brandy
Crushed ice
Orange slices
Maraschino cherries

Mix first 6 ingredients in blender for 3 seconds. Pour into ice-filled glasses. Garnish with orange slices and cherries. Serves 8-10.

LEMONADE

1 C. fresh lemon juice
2 C. cold water
1/3 to 1/2 C. sugar
6 thin lemon wedges

In a pitcher, combine the lemon juice, water, and sugar to taste. Stir until sugar is dissolved, add lemon slices and chill, covered. Makes 3 1/4 C.

HEMINGWAY'S MOJITO

3 fresh mint sprigs
2 tsps. sugar
2 Tbs. fresh lemon juice
1½ oz. light rum
Chilled club soda or seltzer
Lemon slices for garnish

In a tall glass, with the back of a spoon, crush 2 of the mint sprigs with the sugar and lemon juice until the sugar is dissolved. Add the rum. Add ice cubes, top off the drink with the club soda, and stir well. Garnish with remaining mint sprig and lemon slices. Serves 1.

MOSCOW MULE

½ small lime
Ice cubes
2 oz. vodka
4 oz. ginger beer

Squeeze lime juice into an 8 oz. mug (preferably copper if one is at hand.) Add ice cubes, vodka and ginger beer. Serve immediately. Serves 1.

WHITE RUSSIAN

1½ oz. vodka
1½ oz. coffee liqueur
3 oz. half-and-half or milk

Mix liquids and pour over ice. A variation on the theme is called an AGGRAVATION. Substitute Scotch whiskey for the vodka.

KIR

Cold chablis wine
1½ oz. Creme de Cassis

Pour chablis into a large stemmed glass. VERY SLOWLY, add the Creme de Cassis. Do not stir. A very pretty drink. For a Kir Royale, use champagne.

FRENCH 75

1 small lemon
1 tsp. sugar
1 oz. gin
½ oz. orange liqueur
Crushed ice
2 oz. champagne

Remove a strip of lemon zest for garnish. Squeeze 1 Tb. lemon juice into a 6 oz. stemmed cocktail glass. Add the sugar, gin and orange liqueur. Stir until sugar dissolves. Add crushed ice and champagne. Garnish with lemon twist and serve immediately. Serves 1.

    WARNING: This drink was named after a WWI French howitzer with a 75 millimeter muzzle whose "ka-boom" was comparable to that derived from this cocktail!

PISCO SOUR

3 oz. Pisco
1 Tb. sugar
1 oz. lemon juice
1 egg white and crushed ice

Mix the Pisco, sugar, lemon juice and crushed ice. Add the egg white and mix thoroughly. Serve in a cocktail glass.

COFFEE LIQUEUR

4 C. sugar
3 C. water
1/4 C. dry instant coffee
1 C. boiling water
1 vanilla bean
1 quart vodka

Boil sugar and water hard for 20 minutes. Cool. Mix coffee with 1 C. boiling water. Cool. Split vanilla bean in half lengthwise. Drop into half-gallon, dark colored glass bottle. Add vodka. Add cooled mixtures. Store 2 weeks in cool, dark place. Shake occasionally to blend ingredients.

hot under the collar
-soups, gumbos, stew, chili

HOT UNDER THE COLLAR

SOUPS, CHILIS AND STEWS

COLD SOUPS

FRESH FRUIT SOUP

1 quart fresh orange juice
Yogurt, buttermilk, sour cream--any combination thereof to yield
four cups.
1 Tb. honey
2 Tbs. fresh lemon or lime juice
Dash of cinnamon and nutmeg
1½ pints fresh berries or fruit of your choice.
Mint sprigs

Mix together all ingredients except fruit and chill mixture well. Wash and drain fruit as appropriate. Leave whole--blueberries, raspberries, wild strawberries or other small fruit. Slice--large strawberries, bananas, apples. To serve: divide fruit into serving dishes, ladle soup on top. Garnish with fresh mint. Serves 4-6. (Can be used for dessert as well.)

COLD CHERRY SOUP

2¹/₄ C. water
³/₄ C. superfine sugar
3-inch cinnamon stick
4 C. pitted sour cherries, or 2 cans waterpacked sour cherries, drained
1 Tb. cornstarch
2 Tb. water
¹/₃ C. dry red wine
¹/₃ C. heavy cream
¹/₃ C. Cherry Heering, or other cherry flavored liqueur, chilled
Mint sprigs
Whipped sour cream (optional)

Bring water, sugar, cinnamon stick and cherries to a boil. Simmer 30 minutes if using fresh cherries; 10 if using canned. Mix together cornstarch and 2 Tbs. water. Stir into cherries and cook and stir until clear and slightly thickened.

Remove about 1 C. of cherries and some juice; puree in blender and return to rest of soup. Cool, add wine and cream, blend well and chill thoroughly. Just before serving, add cherry liqueur. Serve in chilled bowls garnished with mint and dollops of sour cream.
Serves 6-8.

VICHYSSOISE

3 C. peeled, sliced potatoes
3 C. sliced white leeks
1¹/₂ quarts of canned chicken broth.
Salt to taste.
¹/₂ to 1 C. whipping cream
Salt and white pepper.
2 to 3 Tb. minced chives

immer the vegetables in stock or broth. Puree the soup in blender or food processor, then pour through a fine sieve. Stir in the cream, season to taste, oversalting slightly as salt loses flavor in a cold dish. Chill. Serve in chilled soup cups and decorate with minced chives. Serves 6-8

JANE'S CHILLED CUCUMBER SOUP

1 small to medium onion
1 - 2 cucumbers, peeled, seeded, and coarsely chopped
3/4 C. chicken broth
1 can cream of chicken soup
6 dashes Tabasco
6 dashes Worchestershire sauce
1/2 tsp. curry powder

Blend, chill, and serve garnished with parsley. Serves 4.

CHILLED TOMATO BASIL SOUP

2 1/2 lb. (about 6) tomatoes, cored and cut into chunks
1 Tb. cornstarch
1/2 C. beef broth
1 Tb. fresh lemon juice
1/2 tsp. sugar
10 whole fresh basil leaves plus 1/3 C. chopped fresh basil leaves for garnish
Sour cream for garnish
Extra-virgin olive oil for drizzling on the soup
Garlic baguette toasts (recipe follows)

In a food processor, puree the tomatoes and force the puree through a fine sieve into a saucepan, pressing hard on the solids. In a small bowl stir together the cornstarch and the broth and stir the mixture into the tomato puree.

Bring the mixture to a boil, stirring, remove the pan from the heat, and stir in the lemon juice, sugar, whole basil leaves, and salt and pepper to taste. Let the soup cool and chill it, covered, for at least eight hours. (The soup may be made two days in advance and kept covered and chilled.)

Discard the whole basil leaves, ladle the soup into six bowls, and garnish each serving with a dollop of the sour cream and some of the chopped basil. Drizzle the soup with the oil and serve it with the toasts. Makes about six cups, serving six.

GARLIC BAGUETTE TOASTS

1 large garlic clove, minced or forced through a garlic press
1/4 C. olive oil
1 French baguette, cut lengthwise into six long wedges
coarse salt to taste

In a small skillet cook the garlic in the oil over moderate heat, stirring until it begins to turn golden. Brush the bread wedges with the oil, and on a baking sheet bake them in the middle of a preheated 375° F. oven for 10 minutes, or until golden. Sprinkle the toasts with the salt and break them in half. Makes 12 toasts.

DONNA'S CHILLED BUTTERMILK-BEET BORSCHT

4 large fresh beets
4 C. water
2 tsp. honey
1 tsp. salt
1 medium cucumber
1/2 C. very finely minced scallions
2 C. buttermilk
1 Tb. fresh chopped dill, or 1/2 tsp. dried dill
Fresh black pepper

Peel and quarter beets and place in saucepan with the water and salt. Cook, covered, 15 minutes over medium heat. Cool beets, remove with slotted spoon, and coarsely grate them. Return to the cooking water. Add all remaining ingredients except buttermilk. Mix well, chill until very cold. Whisk in buttermilk before serving. Serve with a garnish of a spoonful of sour cream.

GAZPACHO

1/2 cucumber, peeled
1/2 mild red or white onion
1/2 avocado, peeled, pitted, and diced
1/2 tsp. oregano leaves, crumbled
3 Tb. olive oil
2 Tb. wine vinegar
4 C. canned tomato juice
2 limes, cut in wedges

Cut off a few slices of cucumber and onion and save for garnish. Dice remaining cucumber and onion. Put onion, cucumber, avocado, oregano, oil, and vinegar into a tureen or serving bowl. Stir in tomato juice. Top with reserved cucumber and onion slices. Chill. Ladle into individual bowls. Serves 4-6.

HOT SOUPS

BALINESE CHICKEN SOUP

(Soto Ayam)

This delicious soup is sold by vendors from two-wheeled carts on the Indian Ocean island of Bali.

1 small chicken
Water to cover the chicken
3 quarter-size pieces of ginger root
1 onion, sliced thin
Salt and pepper to taste
4 C. cooked rice
2 C. finely shredded cabbage
1 C. shredded or grated pork cracklings (pork skins, crushed)
4 hard boiled eggs sliced lengthwise into quarters
Hot chili sauce (Try the green Tabasco)

B oil the chicken in the water with the ginger root, onion, salt and pepper until the meat falls easily from the bone. Remove the chicken from the broth, discard the skin and bones and shred the meat.
In a large soup bowl, put a big scoop of rice.
Ladle the hot broth around the rice. Add a large spoonful each of chicken and cabbage to the broth. Place the sliced egg and shredded cracklings on top of the rice. Serve with hot chili sauce on the side. Serves 4.

BRAZILIAN BLACK BEAN SOUP

2 C. dried black beans, well washed
2 quarts hot water
1/2 Tb. salt
1 C. tomato sauce
1 large onion, minced
1 large garlic clove, minced

2 oz. salt pork, diced
1 or more small, seeded, dried red chili peppers (optional)
3/4 lb. pork butt, cubed
1/2 lb. kielbasa sausage, cut into 2-inch lengths
1/4 tsp. freshly ground pepper
Iced orange slices
Watercress sprigs

Soak beans in water for 4 hours. Add salt, tomato sauce, onion, garlic and salt pork. Cover, bring to boil, reduce heat and simmer 45 minutes. Add red pepper, pork, sausage and pepper. Bring back to boil and simmer until beans are tender but still hold their shape. Discard peppers. Adjust seasonings to taste and serve with hot French rolls. Pass iced orange slices and watercress sprigs. For a full meal, serve with kale, collard greens or spinach and plain white rice. Serves 6-8.

TORTILLA SOUP

2 cans Old El Paso tomatoes and green chilies
6 strips bacon, fried and crumbled
1 medium potato, finely diced
1/2 tsp. garlic salt
2 C. water
4 corn tortillas, torn in pieces
4 additional tortillas for garnish
2 avocados, cold and thickly sliced

Cook all together until tortilla pieces are dissolved and potato is cooked. To serve, cut one tortilla per serving into thin strips and put in bottom of bowl. Ladle in hot soup. Drop several slices of cold avocado into soup and serve. Serves 4.

CURRIED CREAM OF CHICKEN SOUP

6 Tbs. butter
2 C. finely chopped yellow onions
2 carrots, peeled and chopped
2 Tbs. curry powder, or more to taste
5 C. chicken stock
6 parsley sprigs
1 chicken, 2½ to 3 lb., quartered; or 6 boneless, skinless chicken breasts (less fat, less bother - cut cooking time to about 10 minutes).
½ C. long grain rice (don't use instant or converted rice)
salt and freshly ground black pepper, to taste
1 C. half-and-half
10 oz. frozen peas

Melt butter in a large pot. Add onions, carrots and curry powder, and cook over low heat, covered, until vegetables are tender, about 25 minutes; stir occasionally. Add the stock, parsley, chicken and rice. Bring soup to a boil, reduce heat, and cover. Cook at a simmer until chicken is done, 25-30 minutes.

Cool chicken in the stock. Remove the meat from the bones and dice it, or dice the breast meat.. Reserve the meat. Pour the soup through a strainer and transfer the solids to the bowl of a food processor fitted with a steel blade. Add 1 C. of the cooking liquid and process until smooth. Reserve the rest of the liquid.

Return pureed soup to the pot and add the half-and-half. Stir in additional cooking stock, about 4 C., until soup reaches desired consistency. Add reserved diced chicken and defrosted peas and simmer the soup for 15 minutes, or until peas are done. Season to taste with salt and pepper and serve immediately. Serves 4-6.

BLUE CHEESE SOUP WITH BACON

6 Tb. sweet butter
2 C. chopped yellow onions
1 leek, white part only, sliced thinly
3 ribs of celery, chopped

3 carrots, peeled and chopped
1 medium potato, peeled and diced
1 C. dry white wine or vermouth
3 C. chicken broth
1/2 to 3/4 lb. blue cheese
Salt and pepper to taste
6 to 8 crisp bacon slices

M elt the butter in a kettle. Add onion, leek, celery, and carrots. Cook covered over low heat until vegetables are tender, about 25 minutes.
Add potato, white wine and broth. Bring to a boil, reduce heat and simmer until very tender, another 20 minutes. Remove soup from the heat and crumble in 1/2 lb. cheese. Stir until cheese has melted. Pour soup through a strainer, reserving the liquid. Transfer the solids to a bowl of the food processor and puree. Mix together with liquid. Serve in soup bowls, garnish with remaining blue cheese. Serves 4-6.

SOUP TORTOLA

2 chicken bouillon cubes
2 chickens, cut up
6 C. water
1/2 onion, diced
2 Tbs. olive oil
Fresh garlic
1 tsp. curry or turmeric
1/2 tsp. nutmeg
Salt and pepper
1 oz. rum
6 scallions or shallots, chopped
3 eggs

B oil chickens in 6 C. water and bouillon. When fully cooked, remove from broth and remove skin. Cool. Fry onions in oil and add to broth along with nutmeg, salt, pepper, rum, garlic and curry. Combine shallots/scallions with eggs. Add slowly to boiling soup and cook 3 minutes. Serves 6. *Jan Robinson, **Ship to Shore*** (see SELECTED READINGS)

MEXICAN BEAN SOUP

1 large onion, chopped fine
1 garlic clove, minced
4 fresh hot green chiles, such as cayenne, each about 4$\frac{1}{2}$ inches long, seeded and chopped
2 Tbs. vegetable oil, plus $\frac{1}{4}$ C. vegetable oil
1$\frac{1}{2}$ tsp. chili powder
1 16 oz. can tomatoes, including the juice, chopped
Two 15 oz. cans pinto beans, drained and rinsed
6 C. chicken broth
6 corn tortillas
2 oz. sharp Cheddar cheese, cut into $\frac{1}{4}$ inch cubes
For the garnish:
$\frac{1}{4}$ C. sour cream
3$\frac{1}{2}$ oz. can chopped green chiles
3 Tbs. minced fresh cilantro

In a kettle, cook the onion, garlic and fresh chiles in the 2 Tbs. vegetable oil over moderately low heat, stirring occasionally for 10 minutes or until vegetables are softened. Stir in the chili powder and cook the mixture, stirring for 15 seconds. Add the tomatoes with the juice, beans and broth, and simmer the soup for 10 minutes.

While the soup is simmering, cut the tortillas in half, stack the halves and cut them crosswise into $\frac{1}{4}$ inch strips. In a skillet, heat the $\frac{1}{4}$ C. vegetable oil over moderate heat until it is hot but not smoking, and in it saute the tortilla strips in batches, stirring, for 15 seconds or until they are crisp and pale golden. Transfer them as they are cooked onto paper towels to drain. Add the strips to the soup and simmer the soup for 3 minutes or until the strips just begin to soften.

Divide the cheddar among bowls and ladle the soup over it. Garnish each serving with a dollop of sour cream, a spoonful of canned chiles and some of the cilantro. Makes about 9 $\frac{1}{2}$ C. Serves 6.

PEANUT SOUP

1/2 C. peanut butter, or 1 C. unsalted dry-roasted peanuts, crushed
2 C. chicken broth
1/2 small onion, finely grated
Dash of Tabasco
Salt to taste
1 C. milk

Place peanut butter in a pot over low heat and gradually whisk in 1 cup chicken broth. Simmer slowly for 10 minutes. Stir in onion, Tabasco, and salt. Simmer slowly for 10 minutes more, stirring occasionally. Stir in milk and second cup of broth, bring to a slow simmer again, stir until mixture is smooth and creamy. If soup is too thick, add more milk and adjust seasoning. If it is too thin, blend in more peanut butter, 1 Tb. at a time. Serves 4.

EASY FRENCH ONION SOUP

5 C. yellow onions, sliced
3 Tbs. butter
1 Tb. olive oil
1 tsp. salt
1/2 tsp. sugar
3 Tb. flour
4 cans beef bouillon
1/2 C. dry vermouth
Salt and pepper to taste
8 slices toasted French or country-style bread
8 bread-sized slices of Swiss or mozzarella cheese

Cook onions, covered, in oil and butter over low heat until soft, about 15 minutes. Increase heat, add salt and sugar, cook uncovered until onions begin to caramelize, about 30-40 minutes. Blend in flour and cook 3-5 minutes until smooth. Add bouillon, vermouth, salt and pepper. Simmer 25-30 minutes more. Put cheese on toast, place in broiler until cheese begins to melt. Pour soup in bowls, top with toast and cheese. Serves 8.

PUMPKIN SOUP

2 1-lb. cans of pumpkin
4 cans chicken broth
2 carrots, chopped
1 stalk celery, chopped
3 slices bacon, diced
1 onion, chopped
1 green pepper, chopped
1 Tb. flour, mixed with water to form a paste
1/2 tsp. thyme
1 C. chopped canned or fresh tomatoes
Salt and pepper
1 C. half-and-half or evaporated milk
1 can beef broth
1/4 C. sherry

In a Dutch oven, heat pumpkin with chicken broth to form a thick puree. Add vegetables and simmer until tender. Add flour, thyme, tomatoes and salt and pepper to taste. Add half-and-half or evaporated milk. Add beef broth to achieve desired consistency. Add sherry and simmer for a few minutes. Sprinkle with fresh parsley if desired. Serves 8-10.

CURRIED CREAM OF MUSHROOM SOUP

4 Tbs. butter
1 Tb. olive oil
8 oz. sliced fresh mushrooms
1 Tb. curry powder
1 tsp. dried thyme
2 family-sized cans condensed cream of mushroom soup
2 soup cans of milk
1/4 C. sherry

Melt butter with oil in a large Dutch oven. Add mushrooms, curry powder and thyme. Saute, stirring, until mushrooms absorb the oil and begin to release it. Add soup and milk and stir until well-blended.

Bring to a near boil, reduce heat, add sherry and simmer for a few minutes. Serves 16. *Church Street Crossing, Black Mountain, NC*

TOMATO BASIL BISQUE

1 stick butter
2 cans Hunt's Choice Cut diced tomatoes with Italian Herbs
2 cans Hunt's Choice Cut diced tomatoes with Roasted Garlic
2 family-sized cans of condensed cream of tomato soup
2 soup cans of milk
1/2 tsp. curry powder
1/4 tsp. ground allspice
2 Tb. dried basil
1/4 C. sherry

Melt butter in large Dutch oven. Add tomatoes, soup, and milk. Stir until well-blended. Add curry powder, allspice and basil. Stir over heat until near a boil. Reduce heat, add sherry and simmer for a few minutes. Serves 16. *Church Street Crossing, Black Mountain, NC*

POTATO SOUP

2 C. sliced onions
1/4 C. butter
2 C. diced potatoes
1 carrot, diced
1 rib celery, diced
6 Maggi vegetarian vegetable bouillon cubes dissolved in 6 C. water
1 bay leaf
1/2 tsp. oregano
1/4 tsp. paprika
Salt and pepper to taste
1 C. half-and-half
1 C. grated Swiss cheese

Saute onions in butter until soft, add vegetables, broth, bay leaf and oregano. Cook until vegetables are tender. Add paprika, salt and pepper to taste. Stir in cream and Swiss cheese until melted.

SHRIMP AND OYSTER GUMBO

2 lbs. shrimp, fresh or frozen
1 pt. fresh oysters
1 C. chopped celery
2 C. chopped onions
1 gallon warm water
1/2 C. cooking oil
1/2 C. bell pepper, chopped
1/2 C. green onion tops and parsley, chopped fine
4 cloves garlic, minced
1/2 C. all-purpose flour
Tony's Seasoning to taste. You can buy it or make it yourself.
See PUP-POURRI section.

Peel and devein shrimp, and season generously with Tony's. Set aside. Using oil and flour, make a roux (see p. 233 for directions.) Pour onion, celery, bell pepper and garlic into roux. Cook slowly in uncovered pot until onions are wilted. Add water and boil slowly in uncovered pot for 1 hour. Add shrimp and cook over medium heat in uncovered pot for 20 minutes. Add oysters with liquid and continue cooking for another 5 minutes. Adjust seasoning. Add onion tops and parsley. Serve in soup plates over cooked white rice. Pass the file! (*fee-lay*--ground sassafras leaves) Serves 6.

FISH CHOWDER

1/4 lb. salt pork, diced
1/2 C. celery, chopped
1 large onion, chopped
1/2 tsp. thyme
1 bay leaf
5 C. cold water
2 C. diced potatoes

2 lbs. fish fillet, cut into 1-inch cubes
1 C. milk
1 C. heavy cream
2 Tbs. flour
1/8 tsp. cayenne pepper
Salt and white pepper to taste
1 Tb. fresh parsley, minced

B lanch the salt pork in boiling water for 10 minutes. Drain. In a heavy soup kettle, fry salt pork over low heat for 5 minutes. Add celery and onion and saute until tender. Add thyme, bay leaf, water and potatoes. Bring to a boil. Reduce heat. Simmer covered for 15 to 20 minutes, or until potatoes are tender.

In a separate bowl, blend thoroughly milk, cream and flour. Add to soup slowly. Simmer, stirring constantly, until soup thickens, 10-15 minutes. Add fish and simmer 5 minutes. Season with cayenne, salt and pepper. Garnish with parsley. Serves 8.

NOTE: Chowder can be served immediately or cooled to room temperature and refrigerated until ready to use. Before reheating, remove fish from chowder and set aside. Bring liquid to a simmer, then add fish, stir, heat and garnish, and serve.

OYSTER STEW

1 1/2 C. milk
1/2 C. heavy cream
1 1/2 pints oysters and liquid
1/4 tsp. freshly ground black pepper
Pinch cayenne pepper
1 1/2 tsp. salt
3 Tbs. butter
Finely chopped green onions

C ombine the milk, cream and oyster liquid in a 3-quart saucepan. Warm over low heat. Add the spices and increase heat, bringing the mixture to a boil. Lower heat and add oysters. When the edges curl, remove from heat. Add butter. Garnish with chopped green onions and serve immediately. Serves 4.

OLD-FASHIONED BEEF STEW

2 lbs. beef chuck, cut in 1$\frac{1}{2}$" cubes
2 Tb. lard or cooking oil
2 C. boiling water
1 tsp. Worcestershire sauce
1 clove garlic
1 medium onion, sliced
1 to 2 bay leaves
1 Tb. salt
1 tsp. sugar
$\frac{1}{2}$ tsp. pepper
$\frac{1}{2}$ tsp. paprika
A dash of allspice or cloves
6 carrots
1 lb. (18-24) small white onions

Thoroughly brown the meat on all sides in hot lard or oil, turning often. Add boiling water, Worcestershire sauce, garlic, sliced onion, bay leaves and seasonings. Cover; simmer (don't boil) for 1$\frac{1}{2}$ hours stirring occasionally to prevent sticking. Remove bay leaves and garlic clove.

Add carrots and onions. (If carrots are large, halve and quarter.) Cubed potatoes may be added also.

Cover and cook 30 minutes or more, or until vegetables are done. Remove meat and vegetables. Thicken liquid for gravy if desired.

BEEF AND GUINNESS® STEW

2 onions, sliced
1 garlic clove, minced
1/2 stick (1/4 c.) unsalted butter
1 lb. boneless lean chuck, cut into 3/4 inch cubes
1/4 tsp. dried thyme, crumbled
1/4 tsp. dried crumbled sage
1 bay leaf
1 C. beef broth
1/4 C. Guinness® stout
A *beurre manie* made by kneading together 1 Tb. softened unsalted
butter and 1 Tb. flour
Oven-roasted potatoes as an accompaniment if desired
Minced fresh parsley leaves for garnish if desired

In a flameproof casserole cook the onions and the garlic in 2 Tb. of the
butter over moderately low heat, stirring, until the onions are softened.
Transfer the vegetables to a bowl and reserve them.

Heat the remaining 2 Tb. butter in the casserole over moderately
high heat until the foam subsides and in it brown the chuck, patted dry and
seasoned with salt and pepper. Add the reserved vegetables, thyme, sage,
bay leaf, broth, and Guinness stout. Bring the liquid to a boil and simmer
the mixture, covered, stirring occasionally, for 1 to 1 1/2 hours or until the
meat is tender.

Discard the bay leaf, bring the liquid to a boil, and whisk in bits of
the *beurre manie*, whisking until the sauce is thickened. Divide the stew
and potatoes between 2 heated bowls and sprinkle them with parsley.
Serves 2.

BONNIE'S FAVORITE BURGOO

This catch-all stew has versions all over the world. It is known as Olla Podrida in Spain, and as Mulligan Stew in Ireland. The ingredients are optional and the stew lends itself well to whatever is on hand. Accompanied with cornbread or French bread, it is a great way to serve a crowd.

3/4 lb. lean stewing beef, cubed
3/4 lb. pork shoulder, cubed
3 1/2 quarts water or stock
1 chicken, disjointed
2 1/2 C. peeled ripe tomatoes, quartered
1 C. fresh or frozen lima beans
1/2 diced hot jalapeno pepper
2 diced green peppers, seeds and membrane removed
3/4 C. diced onions
1 C. diced carrot
1/2 C. diced celery
2 C. diced potatoes
1 C. diced okra
1 bay leaf
1 Tb. Worchestershire sauce
2 C. corn, frozen or freshly cut from the cob
Fresh parsley for garnish

Place beef, pork and water or stock in a heavy lidded dutch oven and bring to boil. Reduce heat and simmer about 1 1/2 hours. Add the chicken, bring to boil again, reduce heat to simmer and cook about 1 hour or until the meats falls easily from the bone.

When cooled enough to handle, remove bones from chicken and return meat to pot. Bring to boil again and add all remaining ingredients except for corn and parsley. Simmer the mixture over very low heat for about 45 minutes, stirring frequently as it thickens. Add the corn and simmer about 15 more minutes until all the vegetables are soft. Adjust seasoning, garnish with parsley and serve.
Serves 10-12

PORK, SWEET POTATO AND BLACK BEAN STEW

This is a microwave version, but it works coventionally as well. Just treat it as would any stew.

1 lb. boneless pork shoulder, cut into 1 inch cubes
2 tsp. chili powder
1 tsp. honey
1/2 tsp. salt
1 onion, chopped
2 lbs. sweet potatoes, peeled and cut into 1 inch cubes
1/4 C. fresh orange juice
1 10 oz. can black beans, drained and rinsed
A *beurre manie* made by kneading together 1 tsp. softened butter and 1 tsp. flour
1 Tb. minced fresh cilantro if desired

In a 2 1/2 quart glass casserole combine the pork, chili powder, honey, salt, onion, sweet potatoes, orange juice, and 1/4 C. water. Cover the surface of the pork mixture with wax paper and microwave at high power for 8 minutes. Stir the pork mixture and microwave it, covered with wax paper, at medium power for 15 minutes, or until the pork is just tender. Stir in the black beans and the beurre manie and microwave the stew, covered with wax paper, at medium power for 2 minutes. Stir in the minced cilantro, and salt and pepper to taste. Serves 2

CARBONADA CRIOLLA

(Baked pumpkin with beef, vegetable and peach filling)

This South American stew is a lot of fun and makes a spectacular presentation. Since pumpkins are generally only available in the fall, it is pretty much a thing to do around Halloween.

1 10-12 lb. pumpkin or large winter squash
1 stick of butter, softened
1 C. sugar
2 Tb. olive oil
2 lb. lean beef chuck, cut into 1 inch cubes
1 C. coarsely chopped onions
$1/2$ C. coarsely chopped green pepper
1 clove finely chopped garlic
4 C. canned beef broth
3 medium tomatoes, peeled, seeded and coarsely chopped
$1/2$ tsp. dried oregano
1 bay leaf
1 tsp. salt
Freshly ground black pepper
$1^1/2$ lb. sweet potatoes, peeled and cut into $1/2$ inch cubes
$1^1/2$ lb. white potatoes, peeled and cut into $1/2$ inch cubes
$1/2$ lb. zucchini, scrubbed and cut into $1/4$ inch slices
3 ears of corn, shucked and cut into 1 inch rounds
4 fresh peaches, peeled, halved and pitted, or substitute 8 canned peach halves, drained and rinsed in cold water

Preheat the oven to 375F° . Scrub the outside of the pumpkin. With a sharp knife, cut a 6-7 inch diameter lid out of the top of the pumpkin. Leave the stem intact on the lid to serve as a handle. Lift off the lid and with a large metal spoon, scrape the seeds and the stringy fibers from the inside of the pumpkin and the lid.

Brush the inside of the pumpkin with the soft butter and sprinkle the sugar through the opening. Tip the pumpkin from side to side to adhere the sugar to the butter. Shake out the excess sugar. Replace the lid.

Place the pumpkin in a large shallow roasting pan and bake in the oven for 45 minutes, or until tender but somewhat resistant when pierced with the tip of a sharp small knife. The shell should remain firm enough to hold the filling without danger of collapse.

While the pumpkin is baking, heat the oil in a 6 quart dutch oven over moderate heat. Add the cubes of meat and brown on all sides. Transfer the meat to a platter, using a slotted spoon.

To the fat remaining in the pan, add the onions, green pepper and garlic and cook over moderate heat for about 5 minutes, stirring constantly. Pour in beef broth and bring to a boil over high heat, scraping in any brown bits clinging to the bottom or sides of the pot. Return the meat and any accumulated juices to the pan and stir in the tomatoes, oregano, bay leaf, salt and a few grinds of black pepper. Cover the pan, reduce the heat to low, and simmer undisturbed for 15 minutes. Add the sweet and white potatoes, cover the pan and cook for 15 minutes. Add the zucchini, cover again and cook for 10 minutes. Finally, add the corn rounds and the peach halves and cook, covered, for 5 minutes longer.

Pour the entire contents of the pot carefully into the baked pumpkin, cover the pumpkin with its lid again and bake for another 15 minutes. To serve, place the pumpkin on a large platter and at the table, ladle the carbonada from the pumpkin onto heated, individual serving plates. Serves 6.

CHRISTIANE'S WATERZOOI

This is a traditional Belgian soup that can also be made with fish instead of chicken.

2 lb. chicken
2$^1/_2$ C. chicken broth
2 carrots, cut into fine julienne strips
2 ribs of celery, cut into fine julienne strips
White part of 1 leek, cut into fine julienne strips and rinsed well
$^1/_2$ C. heavy cream
2 large egg yolks
2 Tb. chopped fresh chervil or other fresh green herbs

In a large saucepan of boiling salted water, blanch the chicken for 3 minutes and drain it. In a heavy saucepan just large enough to hold the chicken combine the chicken with the broth (the broth should come about one-third of the way up the side of the chicken). Bring the broth to a boil and simmer the chicken, covered, for 15 minutes or until it is tender. (The steam in the pan will help cook the chicken.) While the chicken is cooking, to a saucepan of boiling water add the carrots and return the water to a boil. Add the celery, return water to a boil, and add the leek. Return the water to a boil, remove the pan from the heat and let the mixture stand.

Transfer the chicken to a heated deep serving dish or bowl, remove and discard the skin and keep the chicken warm, covered with foil. Boil the broth until it is reduced to about 1$^1/_3$ C. In a bowl whisk together the cream and the yolks, add the hot broth in a stream, whisking, and return the sauce to the pan, whisking. Cook the sauce over moderately low heat, whisking constantly until it is thickened slightly, but do not let it boil. Remove the pan from the heat and stir in the chervil and salt and freshly ground pepper to taste. Drain the vegetables in a fine sieve, spread them over and around the chicken, and pour the sauce over the mixture. Serves 2.

CHILIS

CHILI CON CRETE

Created by Jerry Jones as the official entry in a chili cookoff sponsored by a concrete manufacturng company. It is in the Wick Fowlwer / Frank Tolbert tradition.

1/2 lb. ground chuck
1/2 lb. ground pork
1 lb. chuck or round steak cut into 1/2" cubes
1 large onion, chopped
3 cloves garlic, chopped
1 1/2 tsp. salt
1 1/2 tsp. paprika
3/4 Tb. oregano
1/2 tsp. ground cumin
3 oz. chili powder (Gebhardt's preferred)
1 oz. semi-sweet chocolate (secret mystery ingredient)
8 oz. tomato sauce
chopped jalapenos to taste
1 can beer (cheap is fine)
1 C. water
1/8 C. masa harina (optional)

Sear meat, onions and garlic until meat is grayish. Add salt, paprika, oregano, cumin, chili powder and chocolate. Stir until well blended and simmer for a few minutes. Add tomato sauce and jalapenos and blend. Add beer and water, simmer 1 1/2 hours, stirring occasionally.

Make a flowable paste of masa harina and warm water. Stir in and simmer 15-20 minutes longer. Serves 4-6.

YAHOO!

Step 1:
2$\frac{1}{2}$ lbs. beef chuck, cut into half-inch cubes
1 tsp. shortening
1 8-oz. can tomato sauce
1 14$\frac{1}{2}$ oz. can beef broth
1 tsp. onion powder
$\frac{1}{2}$ tsp. ground red pepper
2 tsp. beef bouillon granules
1 tsp. chicken bouillon granules
$\frac{1}{2}$ tsp. salt
1 Tb. chili powder

In a 5-quart Dutch oven, brown beef in shortening (do not drain). Add tomato sauce, beef broth and 2$\frac{1}{2}$ C. water. Combine seasonings and add to beef mixture. Bring to a boil, reduce heat and simmer for 2 hours.

Step 2:
1 Tb. ground cumin
2 tsp. garlic powder
3 Tbs. chili powder
$\frac{1}{4}$ tsp. ground black pepper
  Combine spices and add to chili. Simmer 30 minutes.

Step 3:
$\frac{1}{2}$ tsp. salt
$\frac{1}{8}$ tsp. ground red pepper
1 Tb. chili powder
1 tsp. ground cumin
$\frac{1}{2}$ tsp. onion powder
  Combine spices and add to chili. Simmer 15 minutes. Serves 6.
  A version of this recipe appeared in the Tampa Tribune in the early 1990s.

SCALLOP AND RED BEAN CHILI

2 Tbs. vegetable oil
2 medium garlic cloves, minced
1 large onion, minced
2 Tbs. chili powder
1/2 tsp. ground cumin
1 tsp. dried oregano
1 tsp. ground cinnamon
1/2 tsp. cayenne pepper
2 16 oz. cans stewed tomatoes, drained
2 16-oz. cans kidney beans with 1/2 C. canning liquid reserved
2 medium green bell peppers, cut into small dice
2 lbs. sea scallops, cut into 1/2 inch pieces, or whole bay scallops
Salt and ground black pepper
1 C. sour cream

Mix first 8 ingredients in a 3-quart microwave-safe bowl. Cover with waxed paper and cook on high power until the onion softens, about 6 minutes. Stir in the next 3 ingredients. Cover and cook on high power until mixture comes to a boil, about 12 minutes. (Can be cooled, covered, and refrigerated overnight.

(Bring mixture to room temperature.) Place the scallops around the edge of the bowl; cover bowl with waxed paper and cook on medium power until scallops are opaque throughout, about 15 minutes. Remove from oven and let stand, covered, for 5 minutes. Season with 2 tsp. salt and 1/2 tsp. pepper or to taste.

To serve, transfer a portion of chili to each plate. Top each serving with a dollop of sour cream. Serve immediately. Serves 8.

THAI WON AHN CHILI

2 lbs. beef stew meat
2 medium onions, chopped
3 cloves garlic, chopped
1 Tb. olive oil
4 Tb. chili powder
1 Tb. ground chiles
4 Tb. beef bouillon granules
12 oz beer
1 8 oz. can tomato sauce
12 oz. water
1/2 C. coconut milk
1/4 C. peanut butter
1 chipotle pepper, chopped

Saute beef, onion and garlic over medium heat until browned. Add chili powder and ground chile pepper and stir and fry for 2 minutes. Add beef bouillon granules, stir. Add beer, tomato sauce and water. Mix well, then add coconut milk, peanut butter and chipotle pepper. Stir until peanut butter is dissolved. Reduce heat and simmer, stirring occasionally, about two hours or until meat is tender.

Serve with jalapeno cheese bread, sliced 1" thick, brushed with olive oil and toasted. *A Dr. Dog Original*

OF INTEREST TO MY RABBIT FRIENDS

SALADS

RADICCHIO AVOCADO SALAD WITH WARM MONTEREY JACK

Lemon-Mustard Vinaigrette:
2 Tbs. lemon juice
1 Tb. Dijon-style mustard
Salt and ground black pepper
3/4 C. olive oil
1/2 lb. Monterey Jack cheese, cut into sixteen 2$^{1}/_{2}$ "x 1$^{1}/_{2}$ " slices,
1/4 " thick
2 medium heads radicchio, torn into bite-size pieces, rinsed and spun dry
4 small ripe avocados, cut into large dice

For the vinaigrette, mix lemon juice, mustard, 1/4 tsp. salt, and 1/4 tsp. pepper in a small nonreactive bowl. Whisk in oil in a slow, constant stream; set aside.

Arrange the cheese slices, about 1/2 inch apart, in a circular pattern on a 12-inch microwave-safe plate.

To serve, arrange a portion of radicchio on each salad plate. Top each with a portion of the avocados. Drizzle 2 Tbs. of vinaigrette over each salad.

Cook cheese on medium power for 3 minutes, rotating the plate 180 degrees after 1$^{1}/_{2}$ minutes. Top each salad with 2 melted cheese slices and serve immediately. Makes 8 servings.

HOLY GUACAMOLE!

2 ripe avocados, peeled and diced
1½ Tbs. lemon juice, preferably fresh
1-2 gloves garlic, minced
1 tsp. dried leaf basil, crushed
¼ C. red pepper, finely diced
2 Tbs. of your favorite salsa
1½ Tbs. slivered almonds, coarsely chopped
2 Tbs. thinly sliced green onion
1 Tb. minced cilantro
½ tsp. salt
A dollop of sour cream for garnish

Peel and mash one avocado, mix with lemon juice, cilantro, garlic, basil and salt. Dice the remaining avocado, fold into mixture with red pepper, salsa, green onion, and chopped almonds. Garnish with sour cream. Serve with tortilla chips and fresh vegetables. *The California Avocado Growers Association*

POTATO SALAD WITH SAUSAGE

1¼ lbs. small red boiling potatoes
3 C. beef broth
¾ lb. cooked garlic sausage or smoked sausage, such as kielbasa, cut into ⅓ inch thick slices
1 small onion, minced
1 scallion, sliced thin
2 Tbs. dry white wine
2 Tbs. white wine vinegar
½ C. olive oil
1½ tsp. minced fresh parsley leaves
1 large garlic clove, minced

In a large saucepan combine the potatoes and the broth. Bring the broth to a boil, and simmer the potatoes for 10 to 20 minutes or until they are tender. Drain the potatoes and let them cool until they can be handled.

Peel the potatoes and slice them 1/3 inch thick. In a large bowl combine the sausage, potatoes, onion and scallion. In small bowl whisk together the wine, vinegar, oil, parsley and garlic, and salt and pepper to taste. Pour the dressing over the warm potato mixture, toss the salad gently but thoroughly, and season it with salt and pepper. Serve 4 to 6.

GREEN BEAN AND POTATO SALAD

1 lb. small thin-skinned potatoes
Salted water
1/4 C. olive oil
1 Tb. white wine vinegar
Salt, pepper or seasoned pepper
1/2 lb. small, slender green beans, ends and strings removed, and cut into 1-inch lengths, or 1 pkg. frozen French-cut green beans
2 Tbs. minced onion
Canned anchovy fillets and capers (optional)

In a pan, cover potatoes with boiling, salted water and cook just until tender, about 25 minutes. Drain. When cool enough to touch, peel and dice. Mix with oil, vinegar, salt and pepper to taste. Set aside to cool.

In a pan, cover beans with boiling water and cook uncovered just until barely tender. For frozen beans, cook according to package directions. Drain and at once immerse in cold water to cool. Drain again. Mix beans with potatoes and onion and chill until ready to serve. Garnish, if desired, with anchovies and capers.

MIDNIGHT SUN POTATO SALAD

1 lb. new potatoes, scrubbed, but unnpeeled
Salt and pepper to taste
1 C. sour cream
1/3 C. chopped purple onion
1/3 C. chopped fresh dill

Quarter and boil clean potatoes in Dutch oven filled with cold, salted water. Cook until tender but firm, about 10 minutes. Drain and place potatoes in mixing bowl. Season with salt and pepper to taste, add sour cream, and toss gently. Add chopped onion and dill, toss again. Cool salad to room temperature, then refrigerate at least 4 hours. Correct seasoning and add sour cream if needed before serving. Serves 4.

TRULY GREAT POTATO SALAD

3 lbs. Yukon Gold or red new potatoes
1/2 C. chicken broth mixed with 2-3 Tb. cider vinegar
Salt and pepper
1 medium mild onion, finely diced
1 stalk celery, finely diced
1 small crisp dill pickle, finely diced
3 hard-boiled eggs, diced
2 Tb. minced fresh parsley or cilantro
1 canned pimiento or roasted red pepper
1/2 to 3/4 C. mayonnaise
Strips of canned pimiento
Parsley and/or chives
Sliced or quartered hard-boiled eggs

Boil scrubbed potatoes in their skins in lightly salted water, just until tender, about 10 minutes. Drain, cover pan, and let sit for 5 minutes. Peel while still warm and cut into 3/16" slices. Toss the still-warm potatoes gently in a large mixing bowl with the broth and salt and pepper to taste. Salt the diced onion lightly and add to the potatoes, along with the celery, pickle, eggs, parsley and pimiento. Toss and fold gently to blend flavors. Correct seasonings. When cool, fold in two-thirds of the mayonnaise, saving the rest for garnish.

May be made a day in advance; cover and refrigerate. An hour or so before serving, taste for seasoning and correct if necessary. Turn the salad into serving bowl, frost the top with remaining mayonnaise and decorate with pimiento strips, herbs and eggs. Serves 6-8. *Adapted from Julia Child & Co.*

SALAD NICOISE

3 C. cold, blanched green beans (see instructions for cooking green beans, p. 170.)
3-4 tomatoes
1 C. vinaigrette dressing
1 head Boston lettuce, separated, washed, drained and dried
3 C. cold potato salad (see "Truly Great" above.)
1 C. canned tuna chunks, drained
1/2 C. pitted black olives (imported preferred
2-3 cold peeled and quartered hard-boiled eggs
6-12 canned anchovy fillets, drained
2-3 Tb. minced fresh green herbs

To assemble salad, toss lettuce leaves in the bowl with 1/4 C. vinaigrette and place leaves around edge of bowl. Season the green beans and tomatoes with vinaigrette. Arrange the potatoes in bottom of bowl; decorate with beans and tomatoes, interspersing them with a design of tuna chunks, olives, eggs, and anchovies. Pour remaining dressing over the salad, sprinkle with herbs and serve. Serves 6-8.

ROASTED SWEET PEPPER AND EGGPLANT SALAD

6 large green or red bell peppers, roasted
1 medium (1 lb.) eggplant
6 Tbs. olive oil
3 medium onions
2 Tbs. red wine vinegar or lemon juice
1 tsp. salt
1-2 large tomatoes, cut in wedges

To roast peppers: Place whole peppers in a single layer in a broiler pan and broil, turning frequently, about 1 inch from heat until peppers are blistered and charred on all sides. Then place in a paper or plastic bag and let them sweat for 15-20 minutes. Strip off skin. Cut peppers lengthwise into 4 pieces and remove and discard stems and seeds. If made ahead, cook, wrap airtight, and refrigerate for 1-2 days. Freeze for longer storage.

Cut peppers crosswise into 1/2-inch strips. Place in a large bowl and set aside. Peel eggplant if desired. Slice eggplant into 1/2-inch thick slices. Using about 2 Tbs. of the olive oil, lightly brush both sides of each eggplant slice, then cut into 1/2-inch thick strips. Set strips on a baking sheet and broil, turning frequently, about 4 inches from heat until very soft and well browned, about 20 minutes. Add eggplant to peppers.

Meanwhile, cut onions in half vertically, then lengthwise in thin slices. Heat remaining 4 Tbs. of olive oil in a wide frying pan over medium heat. Add onions and cook, stirring, until soft and golden, about 20 minutes. Add to pepper mixture. Add vinegar, salt and pepper to taste. Mix lightly. Serve, or cover and let stand at room temperature for as long as 4 hours. Garnish with tomato wedges. Serves 4-8.

MARINATED BLACK BEAN SALAD

4 cans black beans, drained and rinsed
1/2 C. olive oil
1/4 C. balsamic vinegar
1 Tb. grainy Dijon mustard
1 medium red onion, chopped
2 medium tomatoes, peeled, seeded, and diced
1/2 C. chopped fresh cilantro
Salt and ground black pepper to taste
1 red onion, thinly sliced for garnish (optional.)

Drain and rinse beans in colander. To make the dressing, in a small bowl mix together the olive oil, vinegar, and mustard. Set aside. Place beans, onion, tomato and cilantro in a large bowl. Drizzle with dressing and toss. Add salt and pepper to taste. Chill in refrigerator before serving. Garnish with onion rings if desired.

GAY'S ORIENTAL SALAD

1/2 C. salad oil
2 pkg. Ramen noodles, uncooked
2 Tbs. sesame seeds
1 C. slivered almonds
1 head Chinese cabbage
1 bunch green onions (4-6 stalks)
Dressing:
1/4 C. vinegar
1/2 C. sugar
2 Tbs. soy sauce

Saute together first four ingredients. Wash, dry and thinly slice cabbage and onions. Add to sauteed ingredients. Mix dressing in a jar and shake well. Pour over salad. (All the dressing may not be needed. Use to taste.)

TWENTY-FOUR HOUR SALAD

1 10-oz. pkg. frozen peas
1/2 lb. diced fried bacon
1/2 head lettuce cut in 1/2-inch slices
1/2 C. chopped celery
1/2 C. chopped onion
1/2 C. chopped green peppers
1 1/2 C. mayonnaise
1/2 C grated Parmesan cheese
1/2 C. grated Cheddar cheese
1 Tb. salt
1 Tb. sugar

Cook peas in water until crisp; drain. Fry bacon till crisp. Drain. Layer lettuce, peas, celery, pepper and onion in large bowl. Combine mayonnaise with salt and sugar. Pour over top. Sprinkle with cheeses and top with diced bacon. Cover and chill overnight.

SPINACH SALAD WITH PINE NUT DRESSING

6-8 C. spinach leaves, or half spinach leaves and half torn butter lettuce
1/4 C. toasted pine nuts (pignoli)
2 Tbs. tarragon wine vinegar
1/4 tsp. each grated lemon peel and salt
Ground nutmeg
1/3 C. olive or salad oil

Wash greens well and chill. In a small frying pan over medium heat, stir nuts until light browned, 6-8 minutes. Set aside. Place spinach/greens in a salad bowl.

In a small bowl, mix vinegar, lemon peel, salt, dash of nutmeg, and oil. Mix in pine nuts. Pour dressing over greens and mix lightly. Sprinkle lightly with additional nutmeg. Serves 4-6.

CAESAR SALAD

2 large crisp heads romaine lettuce
2 large cloves garlic
Salt
3/4 C. best quality olive oil
2 C. best quality plain unseasoned toasted croutons
1 lemon
2 eggs
1/4 C. Parmesan cheese, freshly grated
Worcestershire sauce

For each serving, strip 6-8 whole unblemished leaves of romaine from stalk. Wash gently to keep from breaking leaves, shake dry, then roll loosely in clean towels. Refrigerate until serving time. (Extra leaves can be refrigerated in a plastic bag for later use.)

To season the croutons, puree the garlic into a small heavy bowl and mash to a smooth paste with a pestle or spoon, adding 1/4 tsp. salt and dribbling in 3 Tbs. of the oil. Strain into a medium frying pan and heat just to warm. Add the croutons, toss for about a minute over moderate heat, and turn into small serving bowl. Shortly before serving, squeeze the lemon into a pitcher, boil the eggs exactly 1 minute, grate the Parmesan into another little bowl.

To mix the salad, first pour 4 Tbs. of oil over the romaine and give the leaves 2 rolling tosses, bringing the salad leaves over upon themselves. Sprinkle on 1/4 tsp. salt, 8 grinds of pepper, 2 more spoonfuls of oil, and give another toss. Pour on the lemon juice, 6 drops of Worcestershire, and break in the eggs. Toss twice, sprinkle on the cheese. Toss once, then sprinkle on the croutons and give 2 final tosses.

Arrange the salad leaf by leaf on each large plate, stems facing outward and a sprinkling of croutons at the side. Serves 4-6. *From Julia Child's Kitchen - the original salad created by Caesar Cardini in Tijuana, Mexico*

CHURCH STREET CROSSING CHICKEN SALAD

4 boneless, skinless chicken breast halves
1 stalk celery, diced
1/4 C. sliced almonds
1 golden delicious apple, peeled and chopped
1 Tb. dried tarragon
2 Tbs. chopped cilantro
Salt and white pepper to taste
Mayonnaise

P lace chicken breasts in salted water to cover. Bring to a boil. Remove from heat and allow to set for 20 minutes. Drain, and when cool enough to handle, trim fat and cartilage from breasts. Split breasts horizontally, then into 1/2 inch strips. Cut into 1/2 inch dice.

Place diced chicken in bowl and toss with celery, almonds, apples, tarragon, salt, pepper and cilantro. Add mayonnaise to taste and mix thoroughly. Refrigerate. Serves 8.

YAM SALAD

A pretty and interesting alternative potato salad

1 pound yams, diced
Boiling salted water
4 large scallions, finely sliced (including the green tops)
2 Tbs. grated or finely minced onion
1 C. finely chopped ripe tomato, peeled if desired
Mayonnaise
Salt and freshly grated black pepper to taste.

C ook the diced yams in boiling salted water until just firm-tender. Drain well and chill, covered, about 1 hour. In a serving bowl, gently but thoroughly combine the yams with all but about 1 Tb. of the scallions, the onion, tomatoe, mayonnaise enough to bind the salad, salt and black pepper.

Arrange the salad in a neat mound, cover, and chill thoroughly. Before serving, sprinkle with the reserved 1 Tb. of scallions. Serves 3-4.
Alex Hawkes, The Flavors of the Caribbean and South America

GARBANZO BEAN, SPINACH AND AVOCADO SALAD

16-oz. can garbanzo beans (chickpeas), drained
5 Tbs. wine vinegar
1/4 C. olive oil
1/2 tsp. salt
1/4 tsp. paprika
1/4 tsp. or more oregano
Dash or more hot pepper sauce
1/2 tsp. minced garlic
1/4 C. minced white onions or scallions
1 pound fresh spinach
3 C. cubed peeled ripe avocado (prepared just before serving)
Salt and freshly ground black pepper to taste.

Place garbanzo beans in a saucepan with the vinegar, oil, salt, paprika, oregano, hot pepper sauce, garlic and onion. Bring to a boil, then remove from heat and allow to cool. Pour into a large salad bowl and chill at least 1 hour.

Thoroughly wash and drain the spinach, trim coarse stems and tear leaves into large pieces. Dry and chill well. Just before serving, add the spinach and the avocado to the chilled garbanzo beans in their sauce. Toss lightly, season with salt and black pepper, and serve at once. Serves 6.
Alex Hawkes, The Flavors of the Caribbean and South America

WEAKLY WILD NEWS

99¢/$1.09 CANADA   70p UK

Extraterrestrials tell Dr. Dog & Jerry their PRIME DISHES are out of this world!!!!!

DR.DOG & JERRY MEET WITH SPACE ALIENS!

Historic rendevous takes place at secret Black Mountain estate

16

0 74851 08101 3

dr. dog's prime

DR. DOG'S PRIME

MEAT, POULTRY AND SEAFOOD

BEEF

ROAST PRIME RIB OF BEEF

5-rib roast
2 Tbs. cooking oil

Preheat oven to 325°F.   Rub the exposed ends of meat with cooking oil and place roast fat side up in a shallow roasting pan.

Put roast in the lower middle level of oven and cook for 2^1/$_4$ to 2^3/$_4$ hours, depending of desired doneness. Every ^{1}/$_2$ hour, check roast and baste with fat accumulated in pan. After 2 hours, begin taking its temperature with an accurate meat thermometer. When it reaches 110°F., the temperature will rise quickly, so keep a close eye on it.

For rosy rare at the large end, the temperature should be 120°F.; the small end will be 125°F. Leave meat thermometer in for 15 full seconds to get an accurate reading. Medium rare: 125°F. on large end and 130°F. on small. Medium: 140°F.. Please do not cook longer than this.

When roast is done, take it out of the oven and place it on a platter or carving board. Let rest for 20 to 30 minutes so juices will retreat back into the meat.

Carving: Slice off one end of roast, turn meat up on that end and slice straight across the top wit a very sharp knife in the English style. Serves 12-16.

ROAST TENDERLOIN OF BEEF

Fully trimmed 4-lb. tenderloin
Meltedbutter
Salt to taste

Preheat oven to 400°F. Brush the roast all over with melted butter and set it fattier (ridged) side up in a roasting dish large enough to just hold it, but not too large. Place it in the upper third level of oven. In 6 to 8 minutes, rapidly turn it and baste it with butter. Turn twice more during roasting, basting with butter, then with accumulated pan juices. After 30 minutes, salt the meat and begin testing for doneness.

Roast will be rosy rare at 120°F and will feel slightly springy when pressed. Remove from oven and let rest 10 to 15 minutes before carving. Serves 6 to 8.

FILET STEAKS WITH MUSHROOM AND MADEIRA SAUCE

6 crustless rounds of white bread
3-4 Tbs. butter
1/2 lb. fresh mushrooms, whole if small, quartered if large
4 Tb. butter
2 Tb. olive oil
2 Tb. minced shallots or green onions
1/4 tsp. salt
Pinch of pepper
6 beef tenderloin steaks (about 6 oz. each, 1" thick)
1/2 C. canned beef bouillon
1 Tb. tomato paste
1/4 C. Madeira mixed with 1/2 Tb. arrowroot or cornstarch
2 Tbs. minced parsley, tarragon and chervil, or parsley only

Melt 3-4 Tb. butter in large skillet, saute bread rounds to brown lightly on each side. Wrap in wax paper and set aside.

Saute mushrooms in 2 Tb. hot butter and 1 Tb. oil for 5 minutes to brown lightly. Stir in the shallots or onions and cook slowly for 1-2 minutes more. Season and set aside.

Dry steaks with paper towels. Place 2 Tbs. butter and 1 Tb. oil in skillet and set over moderately high heat. When foam begins to subside from butter, saute the steaks in it for 4 minutes on each side for medium rare.

Remove from heat. Season quickly with salt and pepper. Place each steak on a bread round and keep warm while preparing sauce.

Sauce:

Pour fat from skillet. Stir in bouillon and tomato paste. Boil rapidly, scraping coagulated cooking juices until liquid is reduced to 2-3 Tbs. Add the starch and wine mixture, boil rapidly for 1 minute to evaporate the alcohol and thicken the sauce slightly. Add sauteed mushrooms and simmer 1 minute more to blend flavors. Correct seasoning. Place the bread rounds on a serving plate, place the steaks on the bread rounds, spread sauce and mushrooms over steaks and sprinkle with herbs. Serves 6.

Adapted from Julia Child, Mastering the Art of French Cooking

FILET STEAKS HENRI IV

6 filet steaks sauteed in oil and butter (see previous recipe)
6 bread rounds (see previous recipe)
1/4 C. Madeira, dry white wine or dry white vermouth
1/4 C. beef canned beef bouillon
6 fresh cooked artichoke bottoms, sauteed in butter, (see p. 170), or canned artichoke botoms.
3/4 to 1 C. Bearnaise sauce (See p. 237)

Saute bread rounds and steaks as described in above recipe. Season steaks and place on rounds. Keep warm in oven.

Pour fat out of skillet, add wine and stock or bouillon, and boil down rapidly, reducing liquid to 3 Tb. while scraping coagulated juices into it. Spoon liquid over steaks. Top each steak with a hot artichoke bottom filled with Bearnaise sauce.

Serving suggestion: Peeled small new potatoes sauteed in butter and parsley and asparagus or green beans, blanched and sauteed briefly in butter. (See p. 170)

AUTHOR'S NOTE: Guaranteed to impress your significant other, married or otherwise. This recipe ensnared my wife. Thank you, Julia Child!

Adapted from Julia Child, Mastering the Art of French Cooking

FILET STEAK WITH JUNIPER MARINADE

6 tenderloins, 8-10 oz.
Hickory chips, soaked in water

Juniper Marinade
1 Tbs. juniper berries
1/4 C. vegetable oil
1 C. dry red wine
3/4 tsp. salt
1/2 tsp. pepper
1/2 tsp. onion powder
1/4 tsp. hot pepper sauce
1/8 tsp. liquid smoke
2 tsp. Worcestershire sauce

P lace a clean towel over berries and crush with a heavy skillet or mallet. combine with rest of ingredients in a glass, ceramic or stainless steel container.

Place steaks in Juniper Marinade, cover and refrigerate for 4 hours, turning once. (A zipper lock plastic bag works great.)

Add the hickory chips to coals five minutes before grilling steaks. Grill steaks 5-10 minutes per side, brushing once with Juniper Marinade Sauce (see below.) Serves 4-6

Juniper Marinade Sauce
        Remaining Juniper Marinade
        1 C. beef broth.

Simmer for 15 minutes, or until liquid is reduced to half. Yields 1 1/2 C.
Adapted from Kokopelli's Cookbook.

GRAND CANYON SUITE

2 4-6 oz. filet steaks
1 large poblano pepper cut in strips
2 Tbs. butter
1 Tb. olive oil
1 C. calabacita or other squash, julienned
2 orange and yellow chiles, julienned
1 medium onion, sliced
1 clove garlic, pressed
1 Tb. cilantro, chopped

Saute poblano peppers in butter and olive oil. Set aside. Saute steaks in same butter and oil. When done, set aside in warm oven. Saute the squash, chiles, onion and garlic until tender firm. Serve steaks with vegetables on side, sprinkle all with chopped cilantro.
A Dr. Dog Original

STEAKS WITH MONTREAL SEASONING MARINADE

One of the best and simplest marinades for steak can be found in a jar of Grill Mates Montreal Steak Seasoning by McCormick.

2 tsp. Montreal seasoning
1/4 C. olive oil
2 tsp. soy sauce

Add 1 lb. steak of your choice to marinade. Let marinate for 45 minutes. Grill and enjoy.

STEAK WITH RED WINE SAUCE

2 small shallots or scallions
4 1 inch thick steaks such as strip, rib eye, or sirloin
Salt and pepper
2 Tb. oil
2 Tb. butter
²/₃ C. red wine

Preheat serving plates in oven set on low heat. Chop shallots. Sprinkle steaks with salt and pepper. In a large frying pan, heat oil over high heat until hot but not smoking. Saute steaks until brown, about 1 minute per side. Lower heat to medium and cook, turning once, about 4 minutes more for medium-rare. Transfer steaks to individual serving plates.

Pour fat from frying pan. Reduce heat to low. Melt 1 Tb. of the butter in pan. Saute shallots until soft, about 1 minute. Add wine, stirring with a wooden spoon to deglaze the bottom of the pan. Bring to a boil and reduce the liquid quickly to a thick, syrupy sauce. Remove pan from heat and stir in remaining Tb. of butter. Season to taste with salt and pepper.

Top steaks with sauce and serve immediately. Serves 4

STEAK DIANE

(Note: This recipe calls for a chafing dish with a strong enough heat source to cook the steaks at the table.)

4 steaks, ¹/₂ inch thick (strips, tenderloin, Delmonico or rib eye)
1¹/₂ Tb. green peppercorns packed in water, or freshly ground pepper
Soy sauce
Olive or peanut oil
Sauce set-up for tableside:
Small pitcher of oil and a stick of butter on a plate
¹/₄ C. each minced shallots or scallions and fresh parsley in small bowls
1 Tb. cornstarch blended with 1 Tb. Dijon mustard and 1 C. beef bouillon in a bowl

Worcestershire sauce
Half a lemon
Cognac and Port or Madeira

Trim all fat from steaks. One at a time, pound steaks between pieces of wax paper to enlarge and reduce thickness to 1/4 inch using a wooden mallet or other appropriate tool. Crush drained peppercorns with back of a spoon and spread a little on one side of each steak, or rub steaks with a grind or two of regular pepper, along with a few drops of soy sauce and oil. Roll each steak into a tube, starting at small end, and place rolls on a platter. Cover and refrigerate until serving time.

Prepare ingredients for sauce set-up. (Can be done several hours in advance. Cover shallots/scallions and parsley with dampened paper towels and plastic wrap, refrigerate bouillon mixture.)

To serve, preheat frying pan in the kitchen to a reasonably hot temperature and bring it and the steaks to the table where the sauce set-up should be ready next to the chafing-dish burner. Saute the steaks two at a time as follows: Pour 1 Tb. oil into the pan as it heats on the flame and add 2 Tbs. butter. Butter will foam, and as foam begins to subside, unroll two steaks immediately into the pan. Saute 30-40 seconds on one side, turn with a fork, and saute on the other side. Rapidly roll them back up and replace on the platter. Cook remaining steaks in same manner.

Add another spoonful of butter, and when foaming stir in a big spoonful of shallots/scallions and parsley, let cook for a moment, then stir in the bowl of bouillon mixture. Stir for a moment, then add a few drops of Worcestershire and the juice of half a lemon. Add droplets of Cognac and Port or Madeira to taste. Finally, unroll each steak and bathe in the sauce on both sides before placing on preheated serving plates. Spoon rest of sauce over. Serving suggestion: Mashed potatoes and fresh or frozen green peas make a hearty accompaniment. Serves 4.

SIRLOIN STEAK WITH BRAISED ONIONS AND BLUE CHEESE

2 Tbs. vegetable oil
2 large red onions, cut into 8 slices
1 C. beef stock or canned beef broth
4 oz. blue cheese, crumbled (1 c.)
1/4 C. dried breadcrumbs
4 sirloin steaks (8 oz. each)
Salt and ground black pepper
2 Tb. Port
2 Tb. butter

Heat the broiler. Heat 1 Tb. oil in a large skillet. Add onion slices in a single layer; saute, turning once, until browned on both sides, about 4 minutes. Add beef stock; bring to boil, cover, and simmer until onions are tender, about 12 minutes. Transfer onion slices to a baking pan; reserve beef stock.

Sprinkle a portion of the blue cheese and then breadcrumbs over each onion slice. Broil onion slices until breadcrumbs are golden brown, about 1 minute; set aside.

Sprinkle steaks with 1/2 tsp. salt and 1/4 tsp. pepper. Heat remaining 1 Tb. oil in the now empty skillet. Add steaks; saute turning once, until seared on both sides, about 5 minutes for medium rare. Transfer each steak to a warm dinner plate; top each steak with 2 onion slices; cover and keep steaks warm.

Meanwhile add port and reserved beef stock to the now empty skillet; bring to boil and cook until reduced to 1/2 C., about 2 minutes. Off heat, whisk in butter, 1 Tb. at a time. Spoon some of this sauce over each steak with onion slices and serve immediately. Serves 4.

PALOMILLA STEAK

3 Tb. butter
1 Tb. olive oil
6 thin sliced boneless sirloin steaks (less than 1/2 in. thick)
2 Tbs. fresh lemon juice
Salt and freshly ground black pepper to taste

In a large skillet, over high heat, melt $1/2$ Tb. of the butter with $1/2$ Tb. of the olive oil. Continuously swirl the skillet until the butter foams and then the foam begins to subside. Place 3 of the steaks with at least $1/2$ in. between each one, in the skillet and saute 1 minute on each side. Remove the steaks to a serving platter and keep warm in the oven while repeating the process with the remaining steaks.

Remove the steaks from the oven and place the remaining steaks on the serving platter. Drain excess grease from pan and discard. Add the lemon juice, salt and pepper and stir over medium heat, scraping up any brown bits. Add remaining 2 Tbs. butter and whisk until melted, then pour it over the steaks and serve. Serves 6.

CHURRASCO

An Argentinian tradition

2 C. finely chopped scallions, or 11/2 C. finely chopped white onion
1 C. plus 2 Tbs. butter
1/2 tsp. crumbled rosemary or oregano, or a combination of both
1/2 tsp. salt
1 Tb. freshly ground black pepper
1 C. dry white wine
1/2 C. wine vinegar or cider vinegar
7 lb. top sirloin steak, or 2 3-1/2 to 4 lb. steaks about 3 in. thick

To make the sauce, saute the scallions or onions in 1 C. of the butter, stirring often. Add the rosemary and/or oregano, salt, pepper, wine and vinegar. Bring to a boil, lower heat, and simmer, 5 minutes, stirring. Correct seasoning and add the remaining butter
Broil the steak over a hot bed of charcoal or gas grill until done to taste: rare, about 40 minutes; medium, 60 minutes; well done 70 minutes or slightly more. Time can vary greatly depending on the heat source. On my gas grill, I allow 30 minutes per side for medium rare. Check with an instant read meat thermometer or by cutting steak open in the middle with a sharp knife. Pour the sauce over the meat for serving. Serves 6 generously.

FAJITAS

"Fajita" in Spanish means "little skirt." A true fajita is made from what is known as a "skirt steak" in Mexico and the Southwestern U.S., the meat skirting the ribs of the cow. Originally, fajitas were marinated to tenderize these tough cuts. Now, other cuts, including flank and chuck are used to create the "sizzlin' fajitas" enjoyed in many restaurants. By the way, there is no such thing as a "chicken fajita." Chickens don't have skirt steaks! However, chickens cooked in this seasoning are "muy bueno!"

FAJITA SEASONING MIX

10 Tbs. chili powder
5 tbs. brown sugar
5 Tbs. onion powder
5 Tbs. garlic salt
5 tsps. Adolph's tenderizer
5 Tbs. paprika
1¼ tsps. celery salt
10 Tbs. MSG
5 tsps. cayenne
7½ tsps. ground cumin
10 tsps. salt
5 tsps. ground coriander
10 tsps. black pepper
1 ¼ tsps. ground nutmeg

Mix thoroughly in food processor or blender.

Fajita Marinade:
1 C. oil
³/₄ C. vinegar
1 ½ C. hot water
½ C. hot water
½ C. lemon juice
⅓ C. soy sauce
4-6 oz. fajita seasoning (above)
Salt and pepper to taste

8-10 lbs. fajita meat

Marinate meat 4-5 hours, overnight if possible. Grill over HOT charcoal until done to your liking. We recommend medium rare to medium, about 7 minutes per side (for beef.) Slice ACROSS the grain into slender strips and serve in warm flour tortillas. Garnish with guacamole, Mexican salsa, picante (not made in New York City) and other Mexican-style condiments.

BEEF BRISKET, TEXAS STYLE

A good smoked brisket is synonymous with Texas barbecue, but it is difficult to do unless you have the right equipment. And unless you are a professional, you probably do not. To properly cook any barbecue requires time, smoke and an indirect fire. Since we live a long way from Texas now, to satisfy that craving for a good mesquite or hickory smoked brisket, I've devised a method that anybody can do.

Marinate a brisket, trimmed or untrimmed, doesn't matter what size, in the fajita marinade described in the previous recipe, or make up your own, or rub the brisket with just the seasoning part. Let it marinate for a couple of days if you have the time.

Light a charcoal fire in your grill or fire up the gas grill, add some soaked mesquite or hickory chips to the fire, and put the brisket on. Try to keep the fire low. I often do this in the evening and let it cook until I am ready to go to bed. Then I remove it from the grill, wrap it in foil, place it in a 200°F. oven (in a pan that will contain any leaking juices) and take it out when I get up the next morning. It will be tender, juicy and delicious.

We developed an interesting variation on this procedure when my daughter came home after we had gone to bed and turned off the oven. In the morning, we arose and gathered our belongings to leave on a several days sailing trip with friends. The brisket was intended as a major food item. Well, of course, it was not at all cooked, but we took it anyway, figuring a way would present itself. It did. As we motored down the Intracoastal Waterway, we put the brisket, well wrapped, on top of the Perkins diesel auxillary engine where it continued cooking to perfection. This procedure is now referred to "Brisket Perkins".

CARNE ASADA A LA TAMPIQUENA

The Meat:
6 pieces of filet steaks, about 6 oz. each, or substitute a thin cut strip
or ribeye steak
1/3 C. orange or lime juice
Salt and pepper to taste

Cut each piece of filet steak if using, horizontallye down to about 1/4 inch of the other side. Continue to butterfly it out to a strip about 1/4 inch thick. Omit this step if using a thin cut steak. Instead, flatten it slightly with a mallet.. Season meat on both sides with juice, salt and pepper. Roll up each piece of meat and set aside to season for about 30 minutes. Meanwhile, prepare the *rajas* and *enchiladas verdes*, below.

To cook the meat, lightly grease the surface of cast iron skillet and place on medium-high heat. When it is very hot, sear the meat on both sides until brown--for medium rare, it should take only 1 minute to cook. Serve immediately with accompaniments below.

The Rajas
6 roasted chiles poblanos (if not available, substitute Anaheims or
other large peppers)
1 medium white onion
4 Tb. vegetable oil
6 cloves garlic, peeled
6 bay leaves
10 peppercorns
2/3 C. cold water
4 Tb. white vinegar
Salt to taste

Over a gas flame or under a broiler roast chiles until well charred on all sides. Place in a plastic bag and let steam for about 15 minutes. Remove and pull charred skin away. Remove the stalks from the chiles, cut off tops, cut them open, and remove seeds and veins. Cut the flesh into strips. Cut the onion in half horizontally and then slice thinly so that you have crescent-shaped slices.

Heat the oil and add the chiles, onion slices, garlic, bay leaves and peppercorns. Cover the pan and cook for about 8 minutes, stirring the mixture from time to time. Add the water, vinegar and salt and cook for a further 5 minutes. Serve hot.

The Enchiladas Verdes

1 can Herdez green tomatillo salsa
4 Tbs. vegetable oil
4 oz. white onions, sliced as for rajas
Salt to taste
1/3 C. oil
12 corn tortillas
4 oz. queso fresco (if not available, use feta)

Heat the oil and fry the tortillas briefly until wilted but not crisp around the edges. Drain on paper towels. Dip each tortilla into the salsa verde, double it over, pour a little more salsa on top, sprinkle with the queso fresco and onion crescents, and serve immediately with the meat and other components.

The Grilled Cheese

1 thick square of panela or other good melting cheese (mozzarella will work).

Sear the cheese, whole if possible, quickly on the griddle until lightly browned.

This combination is a favorite throughout Mexico and in our household as well. It's worth the effort! One serving consists of 1 strip of steak, some rajas, 2 enchiladas verdes, a piece of grilled cheese, a small serving of refried beans (canned will do fine), hot tortillas, and slices of cooling avocado. *Adapted from Diana Kennedy's, The Cuisines of Mexico*

HAVANA STEAK

4 to 6 thin slices sirloin or other good quality lean beef, each about ¼ inch thick.
Juice of 1 or 2 large ripe limes
1 or 2 dashes Tabasco or other hot pepper sauce
3 or 4 Tb. olive oil
¾ C. thinly sliced onions, separated into rings
1 or 2 medium cloves garlic, minced or mashed
½ C. slivered green bell pepper
1 C. finely chopped peeled ripe tomato, salt and freshly ground black pepper to taste
2 to 3 Tb. lard or olive oil
4 to 6 C. hot, freshly cooked white long grain rice
4 to 6 large eggs, fried
2 Tb. minced fresh parsley

If necessary, pound each slice of beef briefly with a meat mallet to tenderize. Place on a plate and sprinkle with lime juice and Tabasco or other hot pepper sauce if desired. Marinate for about 2 hours, turning twice.

Meanwhile, heat the 3 to 4 Tb. olive oil in a skillet over medium heat and cook the onion rings, garlic, green pepper and tomato until soft. Season with salt and black pepper and keep warm.

Drain the marinated beef slices and dry. In another skillet heat the 2 to 3 Tb. lard or olive oil; when very hot, quickly saute the meat, turning only once with kitchen tongs or 2 forks. Spoon about 1 C. of the hot rice on each plate. Arrange meat slices on the rice, spoon on some of the vegetables, and top each serving with a fried egg. Sprinkle with parsley and serve at once. Serves 4 to 6.

THE BEST WAY TO DO A HAMBURGER

2 lbs. good lean chuck, fresh ground
4 Tb. butter (real butter)
1 cast iron skillet

ivide chuck into four portions, using a very light hand. The trick here is to avoid compressing the meat. Shape the portion into disks about 5-6 inches in diameter and about an inch thick. Salt and pepper liberally.

Heat the butter in the cast iron skillet until it foams and the foam begins to subside. Put the hamburgers in the skillet and saute to whatever degree of doneness makes you happy. Serves 4.

This takes the hamburger recipe about as far as it can go, but there are add-ons when you get to the sandwich. This is a favorite at our house:

Saute some onions until they begin to brown. Throw in some sliced mushrooms and cook until they wilt. Put the burger on the bun, top with onions and mushrooms, and add a couple of slices of your favorite cheese. Slip under the broiler until cheese melts.

KEBAB-BURGERS

1 Tb. canola oil
1 small onion, chopped
1 small fresh jalapeno pepper
2 tsps. finely grated fresh ginger
3 cloves garlic, peeled and crushed to a pulp
1 1/2 lb. lean ground beef
1/2 tsp. salt
Freshly ground black pepper

Heat the oil in a non-stick frying pan over medium heat. When hot, add onions, stir and fry until edges begin to brown. Add the jalapeno and stir for another minute. Add ginger and garlic, stir for another minute, then remove from heat.

In a bowl, mix meat, salt and pepper, and mixture from frying pan. Mix gently, but without compacting the meat too much.

Heat large cast iron skillet. Form 4 patties using a light hand, and when frying pan is hot, place patties on surface. When one side is nicely browned, turn the kebab burgers over and brown second side. Turn burgers again, turn down heat and cook to desired doneness. Serves 4.
Madhur Jaffrey's Cookbook

INDIAN BEEF PATTIES IN PITAS WITH CUCUMBER YOGURT

1 oz. ginger root (1-inch cube)
2 large garlic cloves
3 medium jalapenos, seeded and chopped coarse
2 Tbs. fresh mint leaves
1 medium onion, quartered
1 lb. lean ground beef
2 tsp. ground cumin
Salt

Cucumber Yogurt
1 small cucumber, peeled, seeded, and cut into small dice
2 C. plain yogurt
4 large pita breads

For the patties, mince first 4 ingredients in a food processor. Add the onions, pulse until minced. Add the ground beef, cumin, and 1 tsp. salt, pulse to combine.

For the yogurt, mix cucumbers and yogurt in a small bowl. Set aside.

To cook, heat the broiler. Divide ground beef mixture into 8 portions. Form each portion into a thin patty, 3 inches in diameter. Transfer patties to a broiling pan. Broil patties, turning once until they are browned on both sides, about 6 minutes.

To serve, place 2 beef patties into each pita bread. Then spoon a portion of the cucumber yogurt into each pocket. Serve immediately. Serves 4.

See recipe page 188 for making pita bread.

MEATLOAF THIBODEAUX

4 tsp. Tony's Seasoning, prepackaged or make it yourself (see PUP-
POURRI section)
2 bay leaves

4 Tbs. unsalted butter
3/4 C. finely chopped onions
1/2 C. finely chopped celery
1/2 C. finely chopped green bell peppers
1/4 C. finely chopped green onions
2 tsp. minced garlic
1 Tb. Tabasco sauce
1 Tb. Worcestershire sauce
1/2 C. evaporated milk
1/2 C. catsup
1 1/2 lbs. ground beef
1/2 lb. ground pork
2 eggs, lightly beaten
1 C. fine dry bread crumbs

Melt butter in 1 quart saucepan over medium heat. Add onions, celery, bell peppers, green onions, garlic, Tabasco, Worcestershire, and seasoning mix. Saute , about 6 minutes, stirring occasionally and scraping the pan bottom. Stir in milk and catsup. Continue cooking for about 2 minutes, stirring occasionally. Remove from heat and allow mixture to cool to room temperature.

Place the ground beef and pork in an ungreased 9" x 13" baking pan. Add eggs, cooked vegetable mixture (removing the bay leaves), and bread crumbs. Mix by hand until thoroughly combined. In center of pan, shape the mixture into a loaf about 1 1/2 inches high, 6 inches wide, and 12 inches long. Bake uncovered at 350° F. for 25 minutes, then raise heat to 400° F. and continue cooking until done, about 35 minutes longer. Serves 6.

JERRY'S EXCELLENT CHICKEN FRIED STEAK

Cubed beef steaks, one for each person
Salt & pepper
Flour
Eggs, beaten, enough to coat each of the steaks (approx. 2 eggs for every 4 steaks)
Cooking oil

Salt and pepper steaks generously. Dredge in flour, then in the beaten eggs, then in the flour again. If you have time, set steaks on a rack for a short while to let them dry out a little.

Heat about 1/4 inch of cooking oil to very hot but not smoking in a skillet large enough to hold all the steaks. Put in the steaks and brown well on both sides. Reduce heat and cook slowly for 10-15 minutes. Remove to a platter lined with paper towels and place in a warm oven while you make the gravy with the oil from the skillet. See p. 21 for gravy advice.

Serve with some real mashed potatoes (see p. 161) and green peas. This combination is guaranteed to make a statement that would inspire any Texan to stand up and salute the chef.

BEEF STROGANOFF

2 lbs. sirloin steak
2 onions
1 lb. button mushrooms
4 oz. butter
Salt and freshly ground black pepper
1 16 oz. carton sour cream
Fresh chopped parsley

Trim fat off steak and cut steaks into thin strips. Peel and finely chop onion. Slice mushrooms. Melt 2 oz. butter in frying pan, add onion. Saute until softened and add mushrooms. Saute for 2-3 minutes. Drain and keep warm. Add remaining butter to pan, then add steak. Saute on high flame stirring with spoon for 3 minutes or to taste. Put onion and mushrooms in pan, season with salt and pepper. Lower heat and stir in sour cream. Reheat and sprinkle with chopped parsley. Serve over wide egg noodles. Serves 8.

MOUSSAKA

2-3 medium eggplants, sliced about 1/2" thick
2 large onions, chopped
2 1/2 lbs. lean ground beef or lamb
Parsley (handful)
1/4 C. dry red wine
1 C. tomato sauce
Salt and pepper
1/4 tsp. cinnamon
pinch of allspice
2 slightly beaten eggs
1/2 C. grated Parmesan

Bechamel Sauce
1/3 C. butter
1/2 C. flour
2 1/2 C. milk
2 slightly beaten eggs
1/2 C. Parmesan

Saute eggplants in butter until light brown. Drain. Cook onions in 1/4 C. water until soft. Add beef to onions. Stir and cook until crumbly. Remove excess fat. Add parsley, wine, tomato sauce, salt, pepper, cinnamon, allspice and simmer for 10 minutes. Then mix in eggs and parmesan.

To make the Bechamel sauce, melt butter and stir in flour over low heat. Add milk slowly and cook over low heat, stirring constantly until thick. Cool. Them mix in eggs and Parmesan.

In a 10" x 12" pan, layer about 1/3 of eggplant, then add about 1/2 of meat mixture, then a layer of eggplant, the remainder of meat, then the last of the eggplant. Top with Bechamel and sprinkle with more cheese. Bake at 350°F. for 1 hour or until heated through.

MEXICAN CASSEROLE

1¹/₂ lbs. ground beef
1 medium onion, chopped
1 10¹/₂ oz. can condensed cream of chicken soup
1 10 oz. can enchilada sauce
1 10¹/₂ oz. can condensed cream of mushroom soup
1 small can chopped green chiles
1 dozen corn tortillas
¹/₂ lb. Longhorn cheese, grated

B rown meat and onion in a small amount of oil in a skillet. Add chopped chiles, soup and sauce. Cook until well mixed. Place tortillas on bottom of 9" x 13" baking dish. Cover with a layer of meat sauce. Alternate with layers of tortillas and sauce. Should make 2 or 3 layers, ending with meat sauce. Cover with grated cheese and bake at 350° F. for 20 minutes or until cheese is melted. Serves 6-8.

SOUR CREAM ENCHILADA CASSEROLE

1 onion, chopped
2 garlic cloves, minced
3 Tb. vegetable oil
1 lb. ground chuck
1¹/₂ C. bottled or canned green chili salsa
1¹/₂ tsp. dried oregano, crumbled
1¹/₂ tsp. chili powder
1¹/₂ tsp. ground cumin
2 C. fresh or frozen corn
1 Tb. unsalted butter
¹/₄ C. julienne red bell pepper
¹/₄ C. julienne green bell pepper
Six 7-inch corn tortillas
2 C. sour cream
2 C. grated Monterey Jack cheese

1/4 C. sliced pitted black olives

In a skillet cook the onion and garlic in 2 Tb. of the oil over moderately low heat, stirring, until they are softened. Add the chuck and cook the mixture over moderate heat, stirring and breaking up the lumps, until the meat is no longer pink. Stir in the salsa, oregano, chili powder, cumin and salt and black pepper to taste. Bring the mixture to a boil and simmer for 5 minutes.

In another skillet cook the corn in the butter and the remaining 1 Tb. oil over moderately low heat, stirring, for 3 minutes. Stir in the bell peppers and salt and black pepper to taste and cook the mixture, stirring, for 2 minutes, or until the bell peppers are softened. Put 2 of the tortillas, side by side, in an oval 2 quart gratin dish, top them with 1/3 of the meat mixture, 1/3 of the sour cream, and 1/3 of the Monterey Jack. Layer the remaining tortillas, meat mixture, sour cream and Monterey Jack in the same manner, sprinkling the top layer of Monterey Jack with the olives. Spoon the corn mixture around the edge of the dish and bake the casserole in the middle of a preheated 375° F. oven for 20 minutes.

VEAL CHOPS WITH GARLIC AND ROSEMARY

2 eggs
4 veal chops, 1/2 inch thick, with corner bone removed
2 tsp. rosemary, finely chopped
1 C. dry unflavored bread crumbs, spread on a dish
3 Tbs. vegetable oil
2 Tbs. butter
4 garlic cloves peeled and lightly crushed
Salt
Lemon wedges

Beat eggs lightly in a deep dish, until yolks and whites are combined. Flatten the veal chops with a meat pounder. Take one chop at a time, dip it into the beaten eggs to cover both sides. Let excess egg flow back into dish, leaving just a filmy coating on the chop. Sprinkle the chop with the rosemary, then turn both sides of the chop in the bread crumbs to coat. Press the chop flat against the bread crumbs, using the palm of your hand.

Tap it 2 or 3 times, then turn and do the other side. Your palm should come away dry, which means the bread crumbs are sticking firmly to the meat.

Add the oil, butter and garlic to a saute pan large enough to hold all chops, and place over medium high heat. When the butter foam begins to subside, put in the chops. If the garlic has become colored a warm brown, remove it. If it has not, watch it while cooking and remove as soon as it becomes that color. Don't let it burn or turn blackish brown.

When the chops have formed a nice gold crust on one side, turn them. When you have a nice crust on both sides, transfer them to paper towels to drain. Sprinkle with salt, and serve promptly with lemon wedges on the side. Serves 4.

Marcella Hazan, <u>More Classic Italian Cooking</u>

VEAL MARSALA

1 lb. thin veal cutlets
1 sliced lemon
$1/2$ C. flour
$1/2$ C. marsala (sweet sherry)
$1/8$ lb. butter
Salt and pepper to taste

Pound veal until flattened, and cut into 4-inch pieces. Dredge in flour. Heat skillet, melt butter and brown cutlets quickly. Add marsala. cover, simmer on low flame about 5 minutes or until meat is tender. Sprinkle with salt and pepper.

Serve very hot with lemon slices. Serves 4.

SAUTEED PORK MEDALLIONS WITH THAI SAUCE

Thai Paste
1/2 oz. ginger (1/2 in. piece)
1/4 C. plum wine
2 oz. unsalted, roasted cashews
2 Tb. peanut oil
2 medium scallions, sliced thin
1/2 C. loose-packed cilantro
3 medium garlic cloves
1/2 medium chile, such as jalapeno or serrano, seeded and chopped
coarsely
3/4 tsp. turmeric
1/2 Tb. honey
1/2 Tb. sesame oil
1/2 Tb. balsamic vinegar
1/2 Tb. ground cumin
Salt and ground white pepper

4 pork loin medallions (slices of pork loin about 1 in. thick)
Salt and ground black pepper
1 Tb. peanut oil
1/2 C. Tawny Port
1 C. chicken stock or canned chicken broth
1 Tb. lime juice

For the paste, bring ginger and plum wine to boil in a small
nonreactive saucepan; simmer until wine reduces to 1/2 Tb. Transfer
reduction to a food processor; add cashews, peanut oil, scallions, cilantro,
garlic, chile, turmeric, honey, sesame oil, balsamic vinegar, and cumin plus
1/4 tsp. salt and 1/2 tsp. white pepper; process until ingredients form a paste.
Transfer paste to a small bowl; set aside.

Heat oven to 450° F. Sprinkle medallions with 1/2 tsp. salt and 1/4 tsp. pepper. Heat oil in a nonreactive ovenproof skillet. Cook pork medallions over medium-high heat, turning once, until lightly browned on both sides, about 3 minutes. Transfer the skillet to the oven. Roast the meat until the pork is cooked through, about 8 minutes. Transfer pork to a warm plate; cover and keep warm.

Remove and discard all of the pan drippings from the skillet; add port to the now empty skillet. Stirring with a wooden spoon to loosen the browned bits from the bottom of the pan, cook over high heat until the port reduces to $1/4$ C., about 1 minute. Add stock; cook over high heat until liquid reduces to 1 C., about 3 minutes. Whisk in lime juice and $1/4$ C. of the already prepared Thai Paste.

To serve, transfer a pork medallion to each warm dinner plate. Drizzle each with a portion of the pan sauce and serve immediately. Makes 4 servings.

PORK TENDERLOIN WITH CREAM AND CAPERS

1$1/4$ lbs. pork tenderloin
2 shallots
1$1/4$ Tb. butter
Salt and pepper
$1/2$ C. chicken stock
$1/2$ C. heavy cream
2 Tb. capers

Cut the tenderloins into $3/4$ inch thick slices. Mince the shallots. Melt the butter in a large frying pan. Season pork with salt and pepper and saute over medium heat, turning once, until just done but still springy to the touch, about 12 minutes total.

Remove tenderloin, add stock and cream and boil down until fairly thick. Stir in capers. Return tenderloin to skillet and heat through. Serve with boiled potatoes tossed with parsley and butter. Serves 4

CUBAN-CHINESE ROAST LOIN OF PORK

1 4 to 5 lb. pork loin
3 Tb. soy sauce
3 Tb. sherry
2 Tb. hoisin sauce
1/4 C. mashed cooked black beans
2 Tb. Chinese 5 Spice powder
2 Tb. minced garlic
3 Tb. sugar
1/4 C. honey, mixed with 1/4 cup boiling water for basting

Preheat the oven to 425 ° F. Rinse the pork loin and pat dry. Place on a rack in a roasting pan, and fill the bottom of the pan with 1" water. In a mixing bowl, combine the soy sauce, sherry, hoisin sauce, mashed black beans, 5 Spice powder, garlic and sugar. Mix well. Coat the pork loin with the mixture, rubbing the meat all over until the mixture is used up.

Roast the pork 15 minutes, then reduce the heat to 325° F. and cook 1 to 1 1/2 hours, basting every 15 minutes with the honey and water mixture. When the pork is cooked (the inside temperature reaches 160° F. and the juices run clear, not pink), remove it from the oven, let cool slightly, transfer to a serving platter. Serves 6 to 8.

CHIPOTLE PORK ROAST

1 1/2 lb. boneless pork rib roast
Marinade:
     2 chipotle peppers minced
     2 Tbs. minced cilantro
     1 tsp. dried minced garlic
     1 Tb. olive oil
     1/2 C. Madeira

Rub marinade well into the roast and let marinate for up to 6 hours. Roast at 500° for 40 minutes. Add Madeira to pan, scrape bottom of pan to deglaze. Turn oven off, return roast to oven and let sit for 15 minutes before serving. Serves 4.

PORK CHOPS WITH BANANAS AND BACON

4 3/4" thick pork chops
1/2 Tb. dried cumin or to taste
Salt and pepper
1 Tb. butter
4 strips of bacon
2 large bananas
1/2 lemon

Heat the broiler. Sprinkle both sides of the pork chops with cumin, salt and pepper and dot with butter. Put chops in a large, shallow oven proof pan and broil about 6 inches from heat, turning once, about 10 minutes total.

Meanwhile, saute bacon in a frying pan over medium heat until it begins to brown and some fat is rendered, about 5 minutes. Peel bananas, cut them in half lengthwise, and put into a shallow baking dish, cut side down. Squeeze lemon juice over bananas to prevent discoloration. Lay a bacon strip over each banana half and secure with toothpicks at both ends.

Put the bacon and bananas in the oven with the pork chops and continue broiling until the pork is cooked through and the bananas are tender, about 5 minutes more. Serve a pork chop on each plate with a banana half and bacon strip alongside. Serves 4.

PORK CHOPS DIANE

3 pork chops about $3/4$" thick
1 Tb. olive oil
Tony Chachere Cajun Seasoning (See PUP-POURRI)
Thyme
1 cube chicken bouillon
$13/4$ C. hot water
1 Tb. Pick-A-Peppa sauce
1 Tb. instant blending flour or corn starch
$1/4$ C. vermouth
Chopped fresh cilantro (optional)

Sprinkle pork chops with Tony's, place in a medium hot skillet (non-stick preferred). Sprinkle with olive oil and thyme. Saute over medium heat for 5 minutes. Turn, sprinkle with thyme, cover and continue cooking over low heat until done.

Remove chops to warm platter. Deglaze pan with vermouth and allow to boil for about 1 minute. Add bouillon cube dissolved in water, Pick-A-Peppa sauce, flour or cornstarch. When slightly thickened, arrange chops on individual plates, add sauce and garnish with cilantro or other fresh herbs. Serve immediately.

PECAN ENCRUSTED PORK CHOPS

$1/2$ C. light soy sauce
$1/4$ C. lemon juice
2 Tbs. dark brown sugar
4 medium green onions, chopped
2 tsp. prepared horseradish
$1/4$ tsp. grated gingerroot
4 boneless pork chops, at least 1 inch thick
$1/4$ C. flour
$1/2$ C. finely chopped pecans
$1/4$ C. white or yellow cornmeal
1 tsp. salt
$1/2$ tsp. white pepper
$1/4$ C. olive oil

Combine the soy sauce, lemon juice, brown sugar, green onions, horseradish and ginger in a shallow dish. Add the pork chops, turning to coat well. Marinate, covered, in the refrigerator for 1 hour or longer. Drain.

Combine the flour, pecans, cornmeal, salt and white pepper in a shallow dish. Add the pork chops and coat well. Heat the olive oil in a large skillet until hot but not smoking. Brown the pork chops for 5-7 minutes on each side or until cooked through.

We saved this recipe for the end of the "Pork" section, because after you try this, it's likely you'll never cook pork chops any other way!
Atlanta Junior League, True Grits

MONTUNO CUBANO

1½ lb. boneless pork, cut into 1" cubes
Goya Adobo Criollo Seasoning
3 Tb. Goya Extra Virgin Olive Oil
4 lg. cloves garlic
2 lg. onions, sliced
1 pinch of oregano
2 Goya Spanish Pimientos, chopped

Season pork cubes well with adobo. Heat olive oil and brown meat on all sides. Add garlic, onions and oregano. Cook on low heat until onions are translucent. Add pimientos. Serve piping hot with white rice. Serves 4.

LAMB

RACK OF LAMB CASA GRANDE

8-rib rack of lamb
1/2 C. fresh bread crumbs
2 small chiles finely chopped
3 cloves garlic finely chopped
1 1/2 tsp. rosemary
Enough olive oil to moisten the mixture
1 Tb. Dijon mustard

Mix bread crumbs with chiles, garlic, rosemary and olive oil. Brush the fatty side of the rack with Dijon mustard, then pat the bread crumb mixture on top. Roast at 400°F. for 30 minutes for rare.

Rack of lamb doesn't get any better than this.

ROAST LEG OF LAMB

A 5 to 7 1/2 lb. leg of lamb
1 or 2 cloves of garlic
1/3 cup olive oil or cooking oil
Soy sauce
1/2 C. chopped onions
1/2 C. carrots
3 cloves unpeeled garlic
1/2 C. dry white wine or vermouth
1 1/2 to 2 C. or beef bouillon

Preheat oven to 450° F. Remove excess fat from meat. Cut cloves into slivers; make small incisions all over lamb with a knife and insert a sliver into each slit. Massage oil all over surface of lamb. To brown and for a subtle flavor, rub with soy sauce . Recipe can be completed to this point several hours ahead.

Set lamb in middle of preheated oven and roast for 15 minutes. Baste with oil, reduce heat to 350° F. and place vegetables and garlic in the pan. Roast for about 1 1/4 hours. Check with an instant read thermometer. 135° is rare. When the first light pink meat juices begin to exude when the meat is pricked, the lamb is medium rare; when they become a clear yellow, the lamb is well-done.

As soon as lamb is done to your liking, remove to a platter. Skim fat from roasting pan and deglaze pan with the wine. (Pour it in, set over heat, and scrape roasting juices into it.) Transfer ingredients to a saucepan, add stock, and simmer for 20 minutes. Just before serving, reheat and strain into a warm sauce bowl. Lamb is ready to serve in 20 minutes.

BUTTERFLIED LEG OF LAMB WITH CILANTRO MARINADE

Marinate lamb up to one day ahead of cooking.

2 C. dry red wine
3/4 C. soy sauce
1/2 C. extra-virgin olive oil
3 cloves garlic, peeled and minced
1 1/2 C. chopped fresh cilantro
2 fresh or dried bay leaves
1 leg of lamb (6 lb.), boned, butterflied and fat-trimmed
Cilantro sprigs
Salt and pepper

In a 9" x 13" baking dish, mix wine, soy sauce, oil, garlic, chopped cilantro, and bay leaves. Spread lamb open in the marinade and turn to coat. Cover and chill, turn meat ocasionally, at least 4 hours or up to 1 day.

Lift lamb from marinade (reserve marinade) and lay flat (open) on a bar-b-que grill over a solid bed of medium coals or medium heat on a gas grill. Close lid on gas grill. Cook, turning as needed to brown meat evenly, until a thermometer inserted in thickest part is 135°F. for rare, 30 to 45 minutes. Thin portions will be well-done. Brush meat occasionally with marinade up until the last 10 minutes of cooking.

Transfer meat to a platter, keep warm, and let rest for 5-15 minutes. Garnish with cilantro sprigs. Thinly slice meat. Add salt and pepper to taste. Serves 8.

SAUTÉED LAMB CUTLETS WITH 40 CLOVES OF GARLIC

3 Tb. olive oil
40 medium garlic cloves, skin on
1 Tb. minced thyme
4 slices leg of lamb, each ¼ inch thick (1¼ pounds)
Salt and ground black pepper
⅓ C. dry white wine

Heat oil in a large skillet. Add garlic cloves and thyme; cook over medium heat until garlic softens, about six minutes. Remove contents of skillet to a bowl; set aside.

Sprinkle lamb slices with ½ teaspoon salt and ¼ teaspoon pepper. Add lamb slices to the now empty skillet; saute, turning once , until browned on both sides, about three minutes for medium rare.

Remove the lamb from the skillet; cover the meat and keep it warm. Add wine and return reserved garlic cloves and thyme to skillet; simmer this mixture until wine reduces to ¼ cup and forms a sauce, about three minutes.

Transfer a lamb slice to each warm dinner plate. Spoon a portion of the garlic cloves and sauce over each slice. Serve immediately.

SERVING SUGGESTION: Accompany with rosemary roasted potatoes and asparagus.

BALTI LAMB WITH SPINACH

Balti is Pakistani in origin, a marriage of curry and stir-fry.

1 tsp. ginger pulp
1 tsp. garlic pulp
1½ tsp. chili powder
1 tsp. salt
1 tsp. garam masala
6 tsp. corn oil
2 medium onions, sliced

1¹/₂ lb. lean lamb, cut into 2 in. cubes
3 C. water
14 oz. fresh spinach or 1 or 2 packages frozen chopped spinach
1 large red bell pepper, seeded and chopped into bite sized pieces
3 fresh green chilies, chopped
3 tsp. chopped fresh cilantro
1 tsp. lemon juice (optional)

Mix together the ginger, garlic chili powder, salt and garam masala in a bowl. Set aside. Heat the oil in a medium saucepan. Add the onions and fry for 10-12 minutes or until well browned.

Add the cubed lamb to the sizzling onions and stir-fry for about 2 minutes. Add the spice mixture and stir thoroughly until the meat pieces are well coated.

Pour in the water and bring to a boil. As soon as it is boiling, cover the pan and lower the heat. Cook gently for 25-35 minutes without letting the contents of the pan burn. If a lot of water remains in the pan when the meat becomes tender, remove the lid and boil briskly to evaporate any excess.

Meanwhile, wash and chop the spinach roughly before blanching it for about 1 minute in a pan of boiling water. If using frozen spinach, allow to thaw. There is no need to blanch it. Add the spinach to the lamb as soon as the water has evaporated. Fry mixture over medium heat for 7-10 minutes, using a wooden spoon in a semi-circular motion, scraping the bottom of the pan as you stir.

Add the red bell pepper, green chiles and fresh cilantro to the pan and stir over medium heat for 2 minutes. Sprinkle on the lemon juice and serve immediately with plain boiled rice, Naan or Paratha (Indian types of bread.) Serves 4-6.

Shezad Husain, The Balti Cookbook

POULTRY

As you will see from the number of recipes and the many "variations on the theme," chicken--especially the breasts, or "supremes" as they are known in France--is one of our favorite menu items. Cheap, versatile, healthy. Here are chicken recipes from about every corner of the world.

CHICKEN BREASTS WITH TOMATO FONDUE AND TARRAGON

6 boneless chicken breast halves
Salt and pepper
$1/2$ C. flour in a plate
1 Tb. light olive or salad oil
4-5 Tb. butter
1 Tb. minced scallions
3 medium tomatoes, peeled, seeded, juiced and cut into $1/2$ inch strips. (See p. 21 for how to peel a tomato.)
1 tsp. tarragon
$1/2$ C. each dry white wine or Vermouth, chicken stock, and heavy cream
3 Tb. chopped fresh parsley

Season breasts lightly on each side with salt and pepper, dredge in flour, and shake off excess. In a large heavy frying pan or electric skillet, heat 1 Tb. oil and 2 Tb. butter until butter foam begins to subside but has not browned. Add as many breasts as will fit easily into 1 layer. Saute for a minute or two, until lightly browned; turn and saute on the other side only until meat is lightly springy when you press it with your finger. Remove the meat and repeat until all breasts are cooked, adding more oil and butter as needed.

If you wish, flame the breasts in Cognac. Return all breasts to the pan, pour in Cognac, and when bubbling, avert your face and ignite the liquid with a lighted match. Shake pan for several seconds, then pour contents into a side dish.

Add another Tb. or so of butter to skillet, stir in the minced shallots or scallions and cook for a moment. Then add tomatoes and tarragon and cook over high heat for 2-3 minutes more. Then pour in the wine, stock and cream. Boil hard for several minutes until liquids have reduced and sauce has thickened lightly. Taste, correct seasoning, and return breasts to pan to baste in the sauce.

Serve over a bed of rice garnished with parsley, and accompany with a green vegetable or salad. Serves 6.
Julia Child, From Julia Child's Kitchen

CHICKEN WITH GREEN PEPPERCORN MUSTARD SAUCE

2 garlic cloves, minced
1 Tb. unsalted butter
4 skinless boneless chicken breast halves, flattened slightly between
2 sheets of wax paper or plastic wrap
1/3 C. dry white wine
1 C. heavy cream
2 Tb. drained green peppercorns
2 Tb. Dijon-style mustard
1 Tb. snipped fresh chives

In a large ovenproof skillet cook the garlic in the butter over moderately low heat, stirring, until it is softened. Add the chicken, turning it to coat it well with the butter. Cover with a buttered round of wax paper and bake in the middle of a preheated 325° F. for 10 to 12 minutes, or until it is just cooked through. Transfer the chicken to a platter and cover it loosely with foil.

Boil the juices remaining in the skillet until they are reduced to about 2 Tb., add 1/4 C. of the wine, and boil the mixture until it is reduced to about 2 Tb. Add the cream and boil the mixture until it is reduced to about 2/3 C. In a food processor, puree the green peppercorns with the mustard and the remaining wine, stir the mustard mixture into the cream mixture, and bring the mixture to a boil. Stir any juices from the platter into the sauce and spoon the sauce over the chicken. Garnish the chicken with the chives. Serves 4.

CHICKEN EN CROUTE

6 boneless, skinless chicken breast halves
1½ C. chicken stock
½ C. sherry
6 thin slices boiled ham
Dijon-style mustard
Minced fresh tarragon
6 thin slices Gruyere cheese
6 frozen puff-pastry shells, thawed

Poach chicken breasts in chicken stock and sherry for 15 minutes or until tender. Cool and drain. (Save chicken stock for other uses.) Wrap each piece in a thin layer of ham. Coat ham with a thin layer of mustard, sprinkle with tarragon, and then wrap breast in a slice of cheese.

Place thawed puff-pastry shells on a lightly floured surface and roll out each one into a 4-inch circle. Place each chicken breast have on a pastry circle. Position it so that you can fold half the circle over to cover the breast, making a half-moon shape. Wet pastry edges with water, crimp and seal. Place on ungreased baking sheet in 400° F. preheated oven and bake for 20 minutes or until puffed and golden. Transfer to a warmed serving platter and serve immediately. May also be served cold. Serves 6.

CHICKEN SAN MARINO

6 halves boneless, skinless chicken breasts
8 slices Mozzarella or Provolone, ¼ inch thick and cut into 1 x 2½ inch rectangles
8 very thin slices prosciutto
Salt
All-purpose flour
1 or 2 eggs, well beaten
Fine dry bread crumbs
3-4 Tbs. butter
3 Tbs. brandy
½ C. whipping cream

Place chicken pieces one at a time between pieces of wax paper or plastic wrap and pound with flat side of a mallet until about ¼ inch thick. On each flattened piece, lay a rectangle of cheese wrapped in an slice of ham. Wrap the chicken around the ham, enclosing completely. Sprinkle with salt, then coat with flour and shake off excess. Dip each roll in beaten egg, then roll in bread crumbs. At this point, these may be covered and refrigerated overnight.

In a wide frying pan large enough to hold all the rolls, melt 3 Tbs. butter over medium heat. Cook rolls, browning evenly and well on all sides, for about 15 minutes, adding more butter if needed to keep rolls moist. Transfer to an ovenproof serving dish, arranging rolls side by side in a single layer. Bake uncovered in a 350° F. oven for 15 minutes.

To the pan in which you browned the chicken, add brandy. Set aflame, tipping and tilting pan until flame dies. Add cream and boil until large shiny bubbles form and sauce has thickened slightly. Pour sauce over chicken and serve. Serves 6-8. *Sunset, Italian Cook Book*

SWEET AND SPICY CILANTRO CHICKEN

6 boneless, skinless chicken breast halves
1 Tb. olive oil
1 Tb. butter
1 large onion, finely chopped
2 garlic cloves, minced
2 green apples, e.g. Granny Smith, peeled, cored, and chopped
1 Tb. ground coriander
¼ C. chopped fresh cilantro
¼ tsp. ground turmeric
½ tsp. ground ginger
½ tsp. salt
½ tsp. ground cumin
Fresh cilantro sprigs for garnish

Cut the chicken breasts into bite-sized pieces. In a large skillet, heat the olive oil and butter over medium heat. Add the chicken and saute until lightly browned. Add the onion, garlic, apple, coriander, cilantro, turmeric, ginger, salt and cumin. Cover and simmer 10 minutes over medium-low heat. Stir well and serve garnished with fresh cilantro sprigs. Serves 4-6.

GRILLED CHICKEN BREASTS WITH SATAY SAUCE

1/4 C. creamy peanut butter
1 Tb. medium dry sherry
4 tsp. soy sauce
4 tsp. fresh lemon juice
2 tsp. firmly packed brown sugar
1 1/2 tsp. minced garlic
1/4 tsp. Tabasco sauce, or to taste
Vegetable oil
2 boned chicken breast halves, with skin (or not)

In a small heavy saucepan combine the peanut butter, sherry, soy sauce, lemon juice, brown sugar, garlic, Tabasco, and 1/3 C. water and bring the mixture just to a boil over moderate heat, stirring until smooth. Remove the pan from the heat and keep the sauce warm, covered.

Brush a well-seasoned ridged grill pan or cast iron skillet with the oil and heat it over moderately high heat until the oil just begins to smoke. Pat the chicken dry and season with salt and pepper. Place skin side down on pan and grill it, covered, turning once, for 10 minutes, or until just cooked through. Transfer the chicken to a cutting board, let stand for 5 minutes, then cut lengthwise into thin strips. Divide the chicken between 2 heated plates and drizzle it with the sauce. Serves 2.

GOLDEN CHICKEN CUTLETS

6 chicken breast halves, skinned and boned
1/3 C. all-purpose flour
1/2 tsp. salt
1/2 tsp. each: white pepper, ground nutmeg, and marjoram leaves
1 egg beaten with 1 Tb. water
1/3 C. fine dry bread crumbs
1/4 C. freshly grated Parmesan cheese
1/4 C. butter
2 Tb. olive oil
1/2 C. dry white wine
Lemon wedges

Place chicken breasts one at a time between pieces of wax paper or plastic wrap and pound with flat side of a mallet until about 1/4 inch thick. Mix flour, salt, pepper, nutmeg, and marjoram in a shallow dish. Have egg mixture ready in a second shallow dish. Mix crumbs and cheese in a third. Coat chicken breasts lightly with flour mixture, then with egg, and finally with crumb mixture.

Place butter and oil in a wide frying pan over medium-high heat. When butter is melted, add chicken breasts, without crowding, and cook, turning once, until golden brown on each side. Can be served hot or cold, great for picnics or a buffet. Serves 6. *Sunset, Italian Cook Book*

CHICKEN AND MANGO

4 boneless, skinless chicken breast halves
1/2 tsp. salt
1/2 tsp. white pepper
1/2 tsp. freshly ground nutmeg
1 Tb. butter
1 onion, thinly sliced
2 Tb. chutney
1/2 C. white wine
1 ripe mango, sliced
1/3 C. heavy cream

Rinse chicken and pat dry. In a small bowl, mix salt, pepper, and nutmeg. Dredge chicken in seasonings. In a large skillet, heat butter over a moderate flame and saute onion until tender. Add chicken and saute lightly on both sides. Spread chutney on chicken. Add wine to skillet. Cover and simmer for 10 minutes.

Remove chicken to serving dish. Garnish with mango. Add heavy cream to liquid in skillet. Stir and simmer until sauce thickens, about 3-5 minutes. Pour sauce over chicken and mango slices. Serves 4.

CHICKEN ALBUQUERQUE

4 light green chiles, about 3" long, sliced into rings
3 green onions, sliced
2 Tbs. butter
1 Tb. olive oil
3/4-1 lb. chicken tenders
Goya Adobo Criollo
Instant chicken bouillion
1/2 C. Madeira
1 C. cream

Saute chiles and onions in olive oil and butter until they begin to brown. Season chicken tenders with adobo criollo and chicken broth granules. Add chicken to pepper and onion mix and saute until tenders are done. Reserve chicken and vegetables.

Add 1/2 C. Madeira to pan, boil 2 minutes, add 1 C. cream, boil rapidly until thickened. Add reserved chicken and vegetables, heat through. Serves 3-4. *A Dr. Dog Original*

SUPERB SOUTHERN FRIED CHICKEN

1 whole chicken (2 1/2 lbs.)
1 egg
1 1/2 C. buttermilk
1 C. flour
Salt and ground black pepper
1 1/2 qts. vegetable oil

Bring 2 inches of water to boil in a soup kettle. Place chicken on a rack over the water inside the kettle. Cover and steam until chicken is almost cooked, 15 to 20 minutes.

Cool chicken slightly, then cut into 6 serving pieces. Beat egg and buttermilk in a medium bowl. Mix flour, 1 tsp. salt, and 1/2 tsp. pepper in another medium bowl to make seasoned flour. Dip each chicken piece in the buttermilk mixture, then dredge each in the flour.

Heat oil to 365° F. in a large, deep skillet or Dutch oven. Fry chicken over medium-high heat for about 7 minutes. Turn chicken pieces over and reduce heat to medium. Fry until chicken is golden brown, about 7 minutes longer. Drain chicken pieces on paper towels and serve.

CHICKEN SCALOPPINE WITH LEMON

4 boneless, skinless chicken thighs
All-purpose flour
1 Tb. each butter and olive oil
1/3 C. dry white wine or chicken broth
1/4 C. whipping cream
1 tsp. lemon juice
1/4 tsp. thyme leaves
Salt and pepper
Parsley and lemon wedges

Place chiken thighs between pieces of wax paper or plastic wrap and pound with flat side of a mallet until about 1/4 inch thick. Coat chicken with flour and shake off excess.

In a wide frying pan over medium high heat, place butter and oil. When butter melts, add as many chicken pieces as will fit without crowding and cook quickly just until meat is no longer pink when slashed (about 1 1/2 minutes on each side). Place on a hot platter and keep warm. Cook remaining pieces, adding more butter and oil if needed. Add to platter and keep warm.

To pan drippings, add wine and bring to a boil, scraping particles free from pan. Turn heat to high and boil until reduced by about half. Add cream, lemon juice, and thyme. Boil until sauce thickens slightly. Salt and pepper to taste. Pour over chicken and garnish with parsley and lemon. Serves 2.

P. S. CHICKEN

This recipe is adapted from a P.S. in From <u>Julia Child's Kitchen</u>. It became a real favorite with our children and we have always referref to it as P. S. Chicken.

4 boneless, skinless chicken breasts
Herb and lemon marinade:
    1 lemon
    1 tsp. salt and $1/8$ tsp. pepper
    $1/2$ tsp. rosemary or thyme
    1 or 2 cloves garlic, pressed
    $1/4$ C. olive oil
Bread crumbs
Parmesan cheese
2 Tbs. olive oil

Marinate chicken breasts for at least 30 minutes. When ready to cook, wipe breasts with paper towels, then slice into strips. Coast with a combination of bread crumbs and grated Parmesan cheese, then saute them in olive oil.

MUNCHY, CRUNCHY CHICKEN STRIPS

4 chicken breasts, boned, skinned, and sliced into strips
$1/3$ C. soy sauce
$1/2$ tsp. rosemary
1 tsp. garlic powder
1 tsp. each salt and black pepper
2 onions, chopped fine
$1/2$ tsp. ginger
1 C. flour
1 C. oil

Marinate chicken strips for at least an hour, perhaps even over night, in soy sauce, rosemary, garlic powder, black pepper, chopped onions and ginger. Place chicken strips in a deep bowl, powder with flour

n a skillet and fry the strips until they're crispy and

CKEN

3 lbs. .cken, de-boned and cut into bite-sized pieces
1 medium onion, chopped
$1/2$ tsp. thyme
1 medium tomato (optional), peeled and chopped
Salt and pepper to taste
$1/2$ Tb. wine vinegar
2 cloves garlic, minced
3 heaping Tb. curry powder
1 Tb. oil
1 tsp. cumin seed

Combine onion, thyme, tomato, salt, pepper, vinegar, 1 clove garlic, and 2 Tb. curry powder. Place chicken in these seasonings and let stand for 2-3 hours.

Heat oil over moderately high heat in a cast iron skillet. Add the cumin seed and the other clove of garlic, and cook until dark brown. Add remaining Tb. of curry powder and stir. Add the marinated chicken pieces. Cook until chicken is well browned, then lower the temperature and cook until chicken is tender. Serve on a bed of rice.

CHICKEN ENCHILADAS COSTA RICA

1/2 to 3/4 C. finely chopped seasoned cooked chicken
1/2 C. finely chopped pitted or stuffed Spanish green olives
1/2 C. seedless raisins, plumped in boiling water and drained
12 flour tortillas
2 large eggs, lightly beaten
1/2 C. lard
2 Tb. olive oil
1 C. finely chopped onion
1 1/2 C. finely chopped green bell pepper
2 C. coarsely chopped ripe peeled tomatoes
Chopped seeded red chile peppers or hot sauce to taste
Shredded sharp cheese
Minced small white onion or finely sliced green scallion tops
Shredded crisp lettuce

Thoroughly but gently combine the chicken, olives and raisins in a bowl. Dip the tortillas into the beaten eggs. Divide the chicken mixture evenly among the tortillas, spooning a little down the center of each one, then roll up. Heat the lard in a skillet; when hot, fry stuffed tortillas quickly. Set aside.

In another skillet, heat the oil and saute the onion and green pepper, about 8 minutes, stirring. Add the tomatoes, cover, and continue to cook over low heat, stirring once or twice, until all vegetables are soft and well blended. Add the chile peppers or hot sauce, blend, and simmer a few minutes. Add salt and black pepper. Pour this sauce over the stuffed tortillas and sprinkle with cheese and minced onion or sliced scallion tops. Arrange shredded lettuce around the tortillas and serve hot. Serves 6.

SAUTEED TURKEY CUTLETS WITH CRANBERRY ORANGE GLAZE

1 large egg white
1/2 tsp. salt
1 C. fine dry bread crumbs seasoned with pepper
Four 1/4 inch thick turkey cutlets pounded to 1/8 inch thickness
between sheets of waxed paper
1 C. cranberry juice
2 Tbs. lightly packed brown sugar
2 Tbs. cider vinegar
1/4 tsp. freshly grated orange zest
Vegetable oil for frying

In a bowl whisk the egg white and the salt until the mixture is frothy. In a shallow dish have the bread crumbs ready. Dip the cutlets in the egg white, letting the excess drip off. Coat them with the bread crumbs, patting the crumbs to make them adhere, and transfer the cutlets to a rack set on a baking sheet. Chill the cutlets, uncovered, for 15 minutes.

While the cutlets are chilling, in a small saucepan boil the cranberry juice until it is reduced to about 1/2 C. Add the brown sugar and vinegar and boil the mixture until it is syrupy and reduced to about 3 Tb=. Stir in the zest and keep the glaze warm.

In a large heavy skillet heat 1/4 inch of the oil over moderately high heat until it is hot but not smoking. In it fry the cutlets in 2 batches, turning them once, for 1 1/2 minutes. Transfer the cutlets to paper towels, let them drain, and divide them between plates. Serves 2

TRADITIONAL ROASTED TURKEY

Succulent, moist, perfect every time! Just follow these simple steps:

First, buy a small turkey, ideally not more than 10 lbs. This minimizes the imbalance between light and dark meat and allows for faster roasting and a more accurate estimate of doneness. If feeding a crowd, roast two.

Buy a fresh turkey if possible. You may have to order this ahead of time, and be sure to specify that you do NOT want a self-basting bird.

Roast the turkey unstuffed. The turkey roasts faster and times are more accurate. You can baste your separately cooked stuffing with juices collected from the turkey roasting pan.

Baste the turkey. The cheesecloth method described below works exceptionally well, but however you baste the bird, use real butter and broth for moister white meat.

Use an instant read thermometer. The turkey is done when the thermometer inserted in the thickest part of the white meat registers 160°F. The thigh when pricked at its thickest will yield pinkish-yellow juices.

Take the turkey out of the oven when it's done. A 10 lb. turkey will stay hot enough to eat for at least an hour after it comes out of the oven. Wrap it well in foil and don't carve until just before serving.

10-lb. fresh turkey at room temperature
8 Tbs. (1 stick) unsalted butter, softened
Salt and freshly ground pepper
1/4 C. vegetable oil
1/2 C. chicken stock or canned broth

Preheat the oven to 325°F. Cut off the first joint of each wing and reserve, along with the neck, heart and gizzard if making giblet gravy.

Rub the breast with 2 Tbs. of the butter. Season the breast and main cavity lightly with salt and pepper. Truss the turkey if you wish, although this step is unnecessary if the bird is unstuffed.

Set the turkey breast-side up in a shallow roasting pan just large enough to hold it comfortably. Dampen a 1--by-20 inch square of cheesecloth, double it and drape it over the turkey breast. About 3 1/2 hours before you wish to eat, set the turkey in to roast.

In a small saucepan, melt the remaining 6 Tbs. butter in the oil and chicken stock over low heat. When the turkey has baked for 30 minutes, baste it liberally through the cheescloth with half the butter mixture. Baste again with the remaining butter mixture after another 30 minutes. After another 15 minutes, baste the turkey with the accumulated juices from the roasting pan and repeat every 15 minutes until the turkey is done (when an instant reading thermometer in the thickest part of the breast registers 160°.) Begin checking the turkey for doneness after 2 hours and 15 minutes.

With a bulb baster remove the cooking juices from the roaster and reserve forasting the stuffing. (Be sure to include any juices that have accumulated in the turkey cavity.) Wrap the turkey well in foil and set aside until ready to carve, ideally about 1 hour. This will give you time to cook the stuffing and get other items prepared. Serves 8.

SEAFOOD

YELLOWFIN TUNA WITH MACADAMIA NUTS

Two $^1/_4$ inch thick yellowfin tuna steaks (about $4^1/_2$ oz. each)
2 Tbs. olive oil
1 garlic clove, minced
2 Tbs. chopped fresh basil leaves
$^1/_2$ C. fresh white bread crumbs
$^1/_2$ C. finely chopped salted macadamia nuts
1 egg, beaten lightly with 1 Tb. water
2 Tb. unsalted butter plus additional if necessary
Fresh lemon juice to taste

In a flat dish just large enough to hold the tuna in one layer, let the tuna marinate in the oil with the garlic and the basil, covered with plastic wrap, for at least 1 hour and up to 3 hours. In a shallow dish, combine the bread crumbs and the macadamia nuts and have ready in another shallow dish the egg mixture.

Drain the tuna, dip it in the egg mixture, letting the excess drip off, and coat it with the nut mixture, pressing gently to help the nut mixture adhere. In a skillet heat the butter over moderately high heat until the foam subsides and in it saute the tuna for $1^1/_2$ to 2 minutes, or until it is golden. Turn the tuna carefully and saute it, adding more butter if necessary, for 2 minutes more or until the underside is golden and the tuna is just firm to the touch. Sprinkle the tuna with lemon juice. Serves 2.

OLD WIFE IN CHILI-LIME SAUCE

Old wife is the Caribbean name for queen trigger fish. When not available, use sea bass or other white fish.

2 Tbs. olive oil
4 celery stalks, chopped
1 large onion, chopped
2 C. fish stock, chicken stock or water

1 28 oz. can whole tomatoes (undrained)
2 4 oz. cans chopped green chiles
1/4 C. fresh lime juice
1/4 C. chopped fresh parsley
1 large onion, sliced
1 garlic clove, crushed
2 Tb. dry white wine
Pinch of dried basil, crumbled
Fresh ground pepper
4 whole "Old Wife" or about 2 lbs. total fish
Parsley sprigs for garnish

Heat olive oil in deep large skillet over medium-low heat. Add celery and chopped onion. Cover and cook until soft, about 10 minutes; do not brown. Increase heat, add stock or water, tomatoes and liquid, chiles, lime juice, chopped parsley, sliced onion, garlic, wine, basil and pepper and bring to a boil. Reduce heat and simmer 30 minutes. Add fish and simmer gently until just cooked through, 9-10 minutes per inch of thickness. Transfer to large shallow dish, garnish with parsley and serve immediately. Goes great with yellow rice and stuffed christophenes (see p. 177)

SAM'S MARINATED GRILLED SALMON

Salmon filets, enough for four persons
1/4 C. soy sauce
1 C. vegetable oil
2 jiggers rye whiskey
2 cloves garlic, pressed
1/4 C. brown sugar
2 tsp. salt

Mix the ingredients for the marinade, and marinate the salmon in the mixture, skin on, for at least 6 hours. Grill with skin side down over hot coals about 6 minutes. Flip and grill for one more minute.

BAKED REDFISH

1 5 lb. redfish or other thick, white-fleshed fish
1 C. chopped onions
2 C. chopped celery
4 cloves garlic, minced
2 C. cooking oil
2 cans tomato sauce
1 lemon
2 C. cold water
1 can whole tomatoes
Green onion tops and parsley to taste, chopped
Salt, black pepper, and cayenne pepper

Season fish generously with salt, black pepper, and cayenne. Put in baking dish and set aside.

Put oil in a heavy pot with chopped onions, celery and garlic. Cook over medium heat in uncovered pot until onions are wilted, stirring constantly. Add whole tomatoes and tomato sauce. Cook over medium heat in uncovered pot for 40 minutes or until oil separates from tomatoes. Add 2 C. cold water and season to taste with salt, black pepper and cayenne. Cook over medium heat in uncovered pot for 20 minutes.

Pour this mixture over fish. Bake in 325° F. oven for 30-40 minutes, basting several times with the sauce. When fish is done, cut lemon into thin slices and place on top. Sprinkle with green onions tops and parsley before serving. Serve with rice, a green salad, hot French bread and white wine. Serves 6.

TROUT SEDONA

1/2 stick butter
1/2 poblano pepper, cut into thin strips
2 Tbs. butter
2 trout, 3/4 to 1 lb. each
1/2 C. vermouth

Melt the 1/2 stick of butter in a large skillet. Saute poblano strips until they begin to brown. Remove peppers and reserve.

Salt and pepper cavity of trout. Add the 2 Tbs. butter to the skillet, heat to high heat. Saute fish on high heat, 5 minutes on each side. Remove to platter, place in oven to keep warm.

To pan juices add 1/2 C. vermouth. Boil down to thicken. Spoon sauce onto two serving plates, top with trout, then add poblano strips.
A Dr. Dog Original

HALIBUT PACIFICA

2 1-inch thick halibut steaks (or other fleshy white fish)
1/2 C. vermouth
1/2 C. fish stock or chicken broth
2 Tbs. butter
Fresh herbs if desired

In a lidded skillet large enough to hold halibut steaks, bring to a boil the vermouth, fish stock/chicken broth, and butter. Reduce heat to simmer.

Place steaks in liquid. Cover with a piece of wax paper. Put lid on skillet. Poach fish until just done, about 10 minutes. Do not overcook.

Remove fish from cooking liquid and keep warm. Return the liquid to a boil and reduce until it reaches the consistency of a sauce. Add fresh herbs to sauce, and serve over fish steaks. Serves 2.
A Dr. Dog Original

PAN BAGNAS

Provencal Tuna Sandwiches with Basil and Tomato

$^1\!/_2$ C. red wine vinegar
6 flat anchovy fillets, rinsed, patted dry and minced
2 garlic cloves, minced
1 C. extra-virgin olive oil
Two 8 inch round loaves of crusty bread
2 C. thinly sliced radish
2 C. loosely packed fresh basil leaves
1 C. minced onion, soaked in cold water for 10 minutes and drained well
Three 6$^1\!/_2$ oz. cans tuna in oil, drained and flaked.
4 tomatoes (about 1$^1\!/_2$ lbs), sliced thin

In a bowl whisk together the vinegar, anchovies, garlic, and salt and pepper to taste. Add the oil in a stream, whisking, and whisk the dressing until it is emulsified. Halve the breads horizontally, hollow out the halves, leaving $^1\!/_2$ inch thick shells. Spoon $^1\!/_4$ of the dressing evenly into each half.

Working with one loaf at a time, arrange half the radish in the bottom shell, top it with $^1\!/_4$ of the basil, and sprinkle half the onion over the basil. Arrange half the tuna on the onion, top it with $^1\!/_2$ C. of the remaining basil, and arrange half the tomatoes on the basil. Fit the top shell over the tomatoes. Assemble another pan bagna with the remaining bread, radish, basil, onion, tuna and tomatoes in the same manner. Wrap the pan bagnas in plastic wrap and put them on baking sheet. Top with another baking sheet with 4 to 6 lb. weights on it. Chill for 1 hour. The pan bagnas may be made 4 hours in advance and kept covered and chilled. They are best when they have had time to press together. Serve the pan bagnas cut into wedges. Serves 8-10.

SCALLOPS SEATTLE

1 lb. bay scallops
10 oyster mushrooms (or other mushroom caps)
1 thinly sliced green onion, including top
1 Tb. freshly grated ginger
2 Tb. butter
2/3 C. dry white wine
1 Tb. fresh lemon juice
1 C. whipping cream
Salt and white pepper to taste
1/2 C. grated Jarlsberg cheese
1/4 C. bread crumbs

Melt butter in large skillet. When butter is hot. but not browning, add scallops, mushrooms, green onions and ginger. Saute 2 minutes. Remove from skillet and reserve.

Add wine and lemon juice to skillet, cook, scraping pan until liquid is reduced by half. Blend in cream, continue cooking until again reduced by half. Return scallop/mushroom mix to skillet. Add salt and pepper to taste. Cook until just heated through. Divide into oven-safe ramekins. Top with grated cheese and sprinkle lightly with bread crumbs. Dot with butter. Broil until cheese is melted and lightly browned, and serve immediately. Makes 2 dinner portions or 4 appetizers.
A Dr. Dog Original

SEVICHE

Lime-cooked seafood is known as "seviche." Here are two versions of this delectable treat:

POISSON CRU

1¹/₂ lb. firm-fleshed fish, such as snapper or yellowtail tuna, cut into
¹/₄ inch dice
1 C. strained fresh lime juice
Hot pepper sauce to taste, usually about 6 drops
2 Tb. salt
3 medium tomatoes, coarsely chopped
1 C. grated dry coconut
2 C. chilled shredded lettuce
Crisp crackers or crisp thin slices of toasted bread (unbuttered)

In a non-metallic bowl, combine the diced fish with the lime juice, hot pepper sauce, salt and ¹/₂ C. of the tomatoes. Cover tightly and refrigerate for 12 hours.

About 2 hours before serving, drain off the liquid, add the remaining tomatoes and the grated coconut, and mix well. Cover and refrigerate again.

About 15 minutes before serving, stir in the chilled shredded lettuce, mixing well. Drain and serve with crackers or toast. Serves 4-6 generously.

SEVICHE OF SEA SCALLOPS WITH FRESH ARTICHOKES

8-10 large fresh sea scallops
1 fresh lime
Salt and white pepper
1/2 Tb. minced shallots or scallions
2 Tbs. minced fresh parsley
2 Tbs. flour
2-3 lemons
Artichoke hearts, preferably fresh, although canned will suffice
1 tsp. Dijon-type mustard
1 Tb. raw egg white
4-5 Tb. olive oil
For garnish, watercress or shredded romaine, sliced tomatoes or
cherry tomatoes

Wash and drain the scallops. Dipping a sharp knife in cold water
for each cut, slice them crosswise into pieces 3/16 inch thick. Toss in
a bowl with the juice of the lime, a sprinkling of salt and pepper, the
shallots or scallions and the parsley. Cover and marinate in the refrigerator
for at least half an hour, or until serving time.

Prepare a vinaigrette: For about 1/3 C. dressing, beat 1/2 tsp. salt
with 1 1/2 Tb. lemon juice and the teaspoon of mustard, beat in the egg
white, and then by dribbles, the oil. Taste carefully for seasoning, adding
pepper to taste--dressing should not be to strong or it will mask the taste of
the artichokes.

Line individual small plates with watercress or shredded romaine.
Then arrange slices of artichoke interspersed with tomato around the
edges of the dishes, place a rosette of scallop slices in the center, and add a
dot of tomato on top for accent. Cover with plastic wrap and refrigerate
until serving time. May be prepared up to an hour ahead. Serves 4.
Julia Child, Julia Child & Company

BASIC BOILED SHRIMP

Large pot of water
Crab boil
Salt
2 cut up lemons
1-2 lbs. fresh shrimp in the shell

Throw shrimp into boiling water and boil for approximately five minutes. DO NOT OVERCOOK! Drain and chill. Enjoy!

SALT-ENCRUSTED SHRIMP

1 lb. medium-sized shrimp in their shell. (If you prefer to use larger shrimp, increase cooking time by a few minutes.)
4 C. Kosher salt
1 lemon and/or lime cut into wedges

Preheat oven to 350°F. Rinse and thoroughly clean shrimp. Place shrimp in a medium-sized roasting pan or shallow casserole and press the salt on top. (The salt should totally cover the shrimp.)

Roast shrimp for 15 minutes. Remove the pan from the oven and dig the shrimp out from under the salt. Using a pastry brush or paper towel, brush off any remaining salt clinging to the shells. Serve the shrimp in their shells and let everyone peel their own. Pass the lemon and lime wedges separately. Serve with your favorite shrimp dipping sauce, or Tarragon Aioli Sauce (see p. 236).
Kathy Gunst, Roasting

(O(ONUT fHRIMP

Your guests will line up for this one!

4 Tbs. Tony's Cajun Seasoning (see PUP-POURRI section)
2 eggs
1 3/4 C. all-purpose flour (total)
3/4 C. fresh beer
1 Tb. baking powder
4 doz. large or extra large, peeled (but with tails on) and deveined, about 2 lbs.
3 C. frzen grated coconut, about 6 oz., thawed
Vegetable oil for deep frying
Sweet and Hot Dipping Sauce (see below.)

Place Tony's seasoning in a small bowl. In a separate bowl combine 2 tsp. of the mix with the eggs, 1 1/4 C. of the flour, the beer and baking powder. Mix well, breaking up any lumps.

In a small bowl combine the remaining 1/2 C. flour with 1 1/2 tsp. of the seasoning mix. Set aside. Place the coconut in a separate bowl.

Sprinkle both sides of the shrimp with the remaining seasoning mix. Then, holding the shrimp by the tail, dredge each in the flour mixture, shaking off excess, then dip in batter (except for tail), allowing excess to drip off, and then coat generously with grated coconut and place on a baking sheet.

Heat oil in a deep fryer to 350°. Drop several shrimp without crowding into the hot oil and fry until golden brown, about 1-2 minutes. The batter should be cooked through but the shrimp not overcooked. Drain on paper towels. Serve immediately with:

Sweet and Hot Dipping Sauce

1 2/3 C. orange marmalade (one 18-oz. jar)
5 Tbs. Creole or brown mustard
5 Tbs. finely grated fresh or prepared horseradish
Combine ingredients

TUXEDO SHRIMP

1/2 yellow bell pepper
1/2 red bell pepper
2 Cubanelle peppers (or Anaheim or other long chiles)
1/2 medium red onion, thinly sliced
1 inch cube of ginger, minced.
1 banana, sliced crosswise into 1/4" slices
2 Tb. minced cilantro
1 lb. peeled, uncooked fresh shrimp
1/2 lb. bowtie pasta
Olive oil
Tony's Cajun Seasoning (use prepared or see PUP-POURRI section).

Cut pepper into julienne about 1 1/2 to 2 inches long, saute peppers, onion and ginger in a small amount of olive oil until tender, about 7 minutes. Add banana and saute an additional 3 minutes. Set aside.

Bring a large pot of water to a boil and add pasta, cooking until "al dente." While the pasta is cooking, add a tablespoon of olive oil to the saute skillet. When the oil is hot, add the shrimp and sprinkle with Tony's Seasoning. Saute until just done, 2-3 minutes.

Drain pasta. Add vegetables to skillet with the shrimp and heat through. Add to pasta, along with the cilantro, toss and serve. Serves 4.
A Dr. Dog Original

ANGEL'S DELIGHT

1/2 C. chopped green peppers
1/2 C. chopped red onion
1 Tb. olive oil
1 Tb. butter
1/2 tsp. ground saffron
1 tsp. dried basil
1/2 lb. peeled fresh shrimp, seasoned with Tony's Cajun Seasoning
(see p.)
1/2 C. white wine or Vermouth
1/2 C. whipping cream
Salt and pepper
6 oz. angel hair pasta
Chopped cilantro

Saute the peppers, onions, saffron and basil in the olive oil and butter until the vegetables are tender and onions begin to color. Add the seasoned shrimp. Saute until the shrimp are pink and just cooked through, about 2 minutes. Remove to side dish and keep in warm oven.

While cooking the pasta in large kettle of boiling water until "al dente," deglaze the skillet with Vermouth or white wine by cooking over high heat for 1 minute. Add cream, boil until sauce is slightly thickened. Return shrimp and vegetables to the skillet. Mix to cover shrimp with the sauce. Season to taste with salt and pepper. Serve over angel hair pasta and sprinkle with chopped cilantro. Serves 2.

A Dr. Dog Original

THAI SHRIMP AND SESAME NOODLES

1 lb. medium fresh shrimp, shelled and deveined
1 8-oz. bottle of Newman's Own Light Italian Dressing
2 Tbs. chunky peanut butter
1 Tb. soy sauce
1 Tb. honey
1 tsp. grated peeled ginger root
1/2 tsp. crushed red pepper
8-oz. capellini angel hair pasta
1 Tbs. salad oil
1 Tb. Oriental sesame oil
1 medium carrot, peeled and shredded
1 C. chopped green onions
1/4 C. chopped fresh cilantro for garnish

About 1 1/4 hours before serving, in medium bowl, mix shrimp with Newman's dressing. Cover and refrigerate 1 hour. In small bowl, with wire whisk or fork mix peanut butter, soy sauce, honey, ginger, crushed red pepper and remaining dressing. Set aside. After shrimp has marinated for 1 hour, prepare pasta as label directs and drain.

Meanwhile, in 4 quart saucepan, heat over high temperature salad oil and sesame oil until very hot. In hot oil, cook carrot 1 minute. Drain off dressing from shrimp. Add shrimp and green onions to carrot and cook, stirring constantly, approximately 3 minutes or until shrimp turn opaque throughout. In large bowl, toss pasta with peanut butter mixture and shrimp mixture. Sprinkle with chopped cilantro for garnish. Serves 4.

SEAFOOD CREPES

2¹/₂ tsp. Tony's Cajun Seasoning (see PUP-POURRI section)
4 Tb. unsalted butter
¹/₄ C. finely chopped onions
¹/₂ C. finely chopped green onions
1 Tb. all-purpose flour
1¹/₄ C. heavy cream
¹/₂ lb. lump crabmeat (picked over)
1 lb. peeled crawfish tails
³/₄ lb. peeled medium shrimp
12 crepes (see p. 189)

Prepare crepes up to 2 hours ahead. Combine seasoning mix ingredients in a small bowl and set aside. Preheat serving plates in warm oven.

Melt the butter in a 2 quart saucepan over high heat. Add the onions and saute until they start getting tender, about 2-3 minutes, stirring occasionally. Add the seasoning mix and cook about 1 minute, stirring occasionally. Add the green onions and flour, stirring until flour is completely blended into the butter. Then stir in the cream and bring to a boil, stirring frequently. Add the crabmeat; return to a boil, stirring often and leaving crabmeat lumps intact as much as possible. Reduce heat and simmer until sauce has thickened slightly, about 1 minute, stirring almost constantly. Return heat to high. Add the crawfish and shrimp and cook just until shrimp are plump and pink, about 2-4 minutes, stirring often. Remove from heat and serve immediately.

To serve for a main course, one at a time place 2 crepes on each heated plate. Fill each crepe with a scant ¹/₃ C. filling, then fold crepe in thirds. Spoon a little extra filling on top. For an appetizer, serve 1 crepe per person. These crepes may also be topped with a spoonful of Hollandaise sauce. Serves 6 main dishes or 12 appetizers.

ETOUFFEE

This favorite Cajun style dish can be done with either shrimp or crawfish.

8 tsp. Tony's Cajun Seasoning Mix (used prepared or make your own. See PUP-POURRI section).
1/4 C. chopped onions
1/4 C. chopped celery
1/4 C. chopped green bell peppers
3/4 C. Roux (see p. 233)
3 C. fish stock, or substitute chicken stock
1/2 lb. unsalted butter
2 lbs. peeled crawfish tails or medium shrimp
1 C. very finely chopped green onions
4 C. cooked rice

Combine the onions, celery and bell peppers. Prepare the roux (see PUP-POURRI section). Stir in vegetables and 1 Tb. of the seasoning mix with a wooden spoon. Continue stirring until roux mixture cools, about 5 minutes.

In a 2 quart saucepan bring 2 C. of the stock to a boil over high heat. Gradually add the roux and whisk until thoroughly dissolved. Reduce heat to low and cook until flour taste is gone, about 2 minutes, whisking almost constantly. (If any of the mixture scorches, don't continue to scrape the pan bottom.) Remove from heat and set aside.

In a 4 quart saucepan melt 1 stick of the butter over medium heat. Stir in the crawfish or shrimp and the green onions. Saute about 1 minute, stirring almost constantly. Add the remaining stick of butter, the stock mixture and the remaining 1 C. stock. Cook until butter melts and is mixed into the sauce, about 4-6 minutes, constantly shaking the pan in a back-and-forth motion instead of stirring. Add the remaining seasoning mix, stir well and remove from heat. (If sauce starts separating, add about 2 Tbs. more of stock or water and shake pan until it combines. Serve immediately over rice on pre-warmed plates. Serves 8.

Adapted from Paul Prudhomme, Chef Paul Prudhomme's Louisiana Kitchen

FRIED OYSTER LOAVES WITH GARLIC MAYONNAISE

5 tsp. Tony's Cajun Seasoning (store bought or make your own. See
PUP-POURRI section.)
1½ lbs. medium to large oysters with juices
¼ C. all-purpose flour
¼ C. cornmeal
4 7 inch pieces of French bread, cut from ends of baguettes
½ stick unsalted butter, melted
Vegetable oil for deep frying

Stir 2 tsp. of Tony's Cajun Seasoning into undrained oysters in medium
bowl. Marinate oysters for 2 hours at room temperature.

Blend flour, cornmeal and remaining seasoning mixture in another
medium bowl. Hollow out French bread pieces; do not cut in half. (Reserve soft bread for another use.) Drizzle 1 Tb. butter in each.

Lightly toast both sides of bread under broiler. Spread inside
generously with Garlic Mayonnaise (recipe follows). Heat 2 inches oil in
deep fryer or heavy deep saucepan to 375° F. Drain oysters thoroughly,
discarding all juices. Dredge oysters lightly in seasoned flour mixture
using slotted spoon. Shake off excess flour. Slip oysters into hot oil in
batches (do not crowd) and fry until oysters are crisp and float to surface,
about 1 minute. Allow oil to return to 375° F. between batches.

Transfer to paper towels, using slotted spoon, and drain. Divide
oysters among toasted loaves, tapping ends of loaves on work surface to
compact oysters. Serve immediately. Pass remaining mayonnaise separately. Serves 4.

GARLIC MAYONNAISE

2¹/₂ Tb. minced fresh garlic
¹/₄ stick unsalted butter
2 Tb. minced onion
1 Tb. fresh lemon juice
¹/₂ tsp. salt
¹/₂ tsp. hot pepper sauce (optional)
¹/₄ tsp. freshly ground white pepper
¹/₃ tsp. ground cayenne pepper
1 egg, room temperature
1 egg yolk, room temperature
2 C. vegetable oil

Combine first 8 ingredients in heavy 1 quart saucepan. Saute over medium-low heat until vegetables soften, about 4 minutes. Cool 15 minutes.

Mix egg and yolk in processor or blender 30 seconds. Add vegetable mixture and puree about 15 seconds. With machine running, slowly add oil through feed tube. Stop machine and scrape down sides of container. Continue mixing until mayonnaise is thick and creamy, about 15 seconds. Cover and refrigerate at least 30 minutes.

Adapted from Paul Prudhomme, Chef Paul Prudhomme's Louisiana Kitchen

CRAB CASSEROLE MARILYN

1 14 oz. can artichoke hearts, drained
1/2 C. butter
2 bunches green onions, chopped
6 Tb. flour
1 C. milk
8 oz. cream cheese
2 Tb. mayonnaise
1 8 oz. can sliced mushrooms, drained
1 tsp. salt
1/4 tsp. white pepper
1/4 tsp. cayenne pepper
1/2 tsp. garlic powder
1/4 C. white wine
1 lb. white lump crabmeat, drained
Seasoned bread crumbs
Paprika
1/4 C. sliced almonds

Slice artichokes and arrange in bottom of a 10" baking dish. In a 4 C. measure microwave butter on HIGH for 1 minute. Add onions and saute on HIGH for 3 minutes. Stir in flour and add milk gradually. Cook on HIGH for 3 minutes. Mixture should be thick.

Soften cream cheese in an 8 C. measure on HIGH for 1 minute. Stir in mayonnaise. Then blend in a small amount of white sauce to cream cheese until all is mixed. Stir in mushrooms, salt, pepper, garlic powder and wine.

Fold crabmeat in gently. Pour over artichokes in baking dish. Sprinkle with bread crumbs, paprika and almonds. Cook on HIGH for 4 minutes until heated through. Turn dish one time. Serve on toast points, toasted English muffins or in pastry shells. Serves 6.

pawsta & etc.

"PAWSTA," RICE AND OTHER GRAINS

PASTA

BASIC TECHNIQUE FOR COOKING PERFECT "PAWSTA"

The variety of pastas available today is amazing. When I was growing up, we had spaghetti, macaroni, and noodles. Now, the world is your pasta, so to speak. I recommend buying pasta fresh when you can. Some Italian restaurants sell it by the pound, made fresh daily on premises. The next best option is the fresh-packaged pasta in your supermarket's refrigerated case. Last option, the box. Pasta is pasta, no matter how you boil it. But to use it in any recipe, it should be cooked to a perfect ""al dente" (to the tooth) state, tender but firm, not mushy. The directions on the package should guide you best.

Because there are so many excellent Italian cookbooks available, we are including only a few of our very favorite recipes for pasta in this book. See Selected Reading for a list of truly great cookbooks.)

FETTUCCINE AL CINDY

1/2 lb. fresh fettucini
3 bananas diced
1 serrano pepper diced
1 Tb. mint leaves, minced
2 Tbs. canned pimiento peppers, diced
1/2 stick butter
1/2 C. cream
Lime or lemon juice

Combine bananas, mint leaves and peppers, sprinkle with lime or lemon juice. Cook fettucini until *al dente*. In meantime melt butter, add cream. Add fettucini to butter and cream, and stir in the salsa. Serves 2-4. *A Dr. Dog Original*

FETTUCCINE ALFREDO

1/4 lb. Parmesan cheese (about 1 C. grated) or better yet, grate some
   fresh Pecorino Romano
1 lb. fettucini
1 1/2 C. heavy cream
4 Tbs. butter
Salt and pepper

B ring a large pot of salted water to a boil. While the water is heating, place a large mixing bowl, over the pot and add 1/2 of the cheese, the cream and the butter to the bowl. This will melt and warm the Alfredo sauce. When the water comes to a boil, add the fettuccine and cook until tender, about 10 minutes. Drain and return to pot. Add the sauce and mix well. Stir in the remaining 1/2 C. of the Parmesan cheese and toss again. Season to taste with salt and pepper. Serve immediately. Serves 4.

PASTA RAPIDA

1/3 C. olive oil
2 small, dried hot red chiles, each broken into 3 pieces
2 cloves garlic, minced or pressed
1/2 tsp. salt
1/2 C. chopped parsley
8 oz. packaged medium-wide noodles
Salted water in large Dutch oven or pot

H eat olive oil in a small pan over low heat. Add chiles and cook until they begin to brown. Add garlic and cook for about 30 seconds more or just until limp. (Do not brown.) Add salt and parsley and cook, stirring occasionally, for 1 minute more. Remove from heat.

    Cook noodles in large kettle of boiling salted water until "al dente", (2-3 minutes for fresh noodles, or follow package directions.) Drain well and place on a warm platter. Spoon sauce over noodles. Lift and mix gently, then serve. Makes 4-6 servings.
Sunset, Italian Cook Book

SPAGHETTI BALDUINI

1/2 C. finely diced onions
2 Tbs. olive oil
2 Tbs. butter
1 clove garlic, mashed
1 lb. ripe red tomatoes, peeled and chopped
1/4 tsp. salt
3/4 lb. zucchini, cut in thin strips
3/4 C. olive oil
1 lb. spaghetti
1/2 C. freshly grated Parmesan cheese

In a frying pan, saute onion in the olive oil and butter until it is golden brown. Add the garlic, tomatoes and salt, and simmer slowly for 10 minutes. In another pan, fast-fry the zucchini strips in 3/4 C. of olive oil until zucchini is crisp. While the zucchini is frying, cook the spaghetti in salted water. When the spaghetti is cooked, strain and toss in the frying pan with the sauce, adding the Parmesan cheese. Add the crisp zucchini and serve instantly.

LINGUINI WITH CLAM SAUCE

1/2 lb. linguini
1 can Progresso white clam sauce

Cook linguini until "al dente". Warm clam sauce in saucepan. Ladle the sauce over the linguini and pass the Parmesan.

ANGEL HAIR WITH HERBS

1 lb. angel hair pasta
2 Tbs. butter
1 Tb. olive oil
Fresh herbs of your choice, chopped finely.

Prepare pasta using the basic technique for cooking perfect "pawsta" at beginning of this section. While pasta is cooking, melt butter and oil in small skillet. Place cooked and drained angel hair on warm serving plates, toss with butter/oil mixture, then add herbs and toss again to mix.

PASTA PUTTANESCA

Reputedly a favorite of Italian "ladies of the night", the puttane, this bold dish is not for the faint of heart.

1 lb. spaghetti, linguine or other thin dried pasta
2 lbs. canned crushed tomatoes
$1/4$ C. best-quality olive oil
1 tsp. oregano
$1/8$ tsp. dried red pepper flakes, or to taste
$1/2$ C. tiny black Nicoise or other imported black olives
$1/4$ C. drained capers
4 garlic cloves, peeled and chopped
8 anchovy fillets, coarsely chopped
$1/2$ C. chopped Italian parsley, plus additional for garnish

Prepare pasta using the basic technique for cooking perfect "pawsta" at the beginning of this section. Drain immediately when done and transfer to 4 heated plates.

While spaghetti is cooking, drain the tomatoes and squeeze out as much liquid as possible. Combine tomatoes and olive oil in a skillet and bring to a boil. Keep the sauce at a full boil and add remaining ingredients except pasta, one at a time, stirring frequently.

Reduce heat slightly and continue to cook for a few minutes or until sauce has thickened to your liking. Serve immediately over hot pasta and garnish with additional chopped parsley.

RICE

PERFECT PLAIN RICE

No one should ever have to suffer "instant" rice, when the real thing is so cheap and easy! First, if you have an Oriental grocery anywhere nearby, go there and purchase a large bag of jasmine rice. It smells wonderful, tastes great, and compliments any meal. If you must buy rice at the supermarket, Uncle Ben's or some similar brand will suffice. Don't go for the cheap stuff. It's awful.

Rice is always 2:1. Two cups water, one cup rice. Halve it, double it. That's the measure. Wash the rice to remove as much "flour" as you can. Add rice to water and bring to a boil, add 1 Tb. olive oil or butter to 2 C. of water (another reliable relationship when it comes to rice.) I also add either 1 tsp. salt or a cube of chicken bouillon. Depending on your intended use, add basil, tarragon, or allspice. Get creative. Rice offers many opportunities for experimentation.

Simmer on low, covered tightly for 20 minutes. No more. No less. If you're worried about rice sticking to the pan, spray the pan with non-stick vegetable coating before you start your rice.

PAT'S LEMON PILAF

1 C. celery, chopped
1 C. green onions with tops, sliced
2 Tbs. butter or margarine
3 C. cooked rice
1 Tb. lemon peel, grated
1 tsp. salt
1/4 tsp. pepper

Saute celery and onions in butter until tender. Add rice, lemon peel and seasonings; toss lightly. Continue cooking over low heat about 2 minutes or until thoroughly heated, stirring occasionally. Serve with broiled chicken, breast of veal, or baked or broiled fish and your choice of condiments such as raisins, chutney, sliced almonds, toasted coconut or crisp crumbled bacon. Also good with Cornish hen. Serves 6.

SPANISH RICE

2 C. rice
6 Tbs. lard, butter or margarine
2 small onions, finely chopped
2 cloves garlic, minced or pressed
1 C. tomato puree
4 C. beef or chicken broth
2 or 3 canned green chiles, or fresh green chiles,
    seeded and chopped
2 Tbs. chopped fresh cilantro
1 C. pimiento-stuffed green olives

In a wide frying pan over medium high heat, brown rice lightly in lard. Add onion, garlic, and tomato, and cook for 2 or 3 minutes; add 3 C. of the broth and chiles, if used.

Cover and simmer 25 to 35 minutes or bake, covered, in a 350° F. oven 50 to 60 minutes. Add more broth, if needed, to cook rice, however, there should be no liquid remaining when rice is tender. Add cilantro during last 10 minutes. Garnish rice with olives. Serves 6.

SEAFOOD DIRTY RICE

1 3/4 lbs. small shrimp with heads and shells
2 Tbs. unsalted butter
1 Tb. vegetable oil
1/2 C. canned tomato sauce
3 Tbs. onions, finely chopped
2 1/2 Tbs. green bell peppers, finely chopped
2 Tbs. celery, finely chopped
1 tsp. minced garlic
1 tsp. salt
1 tsp. white pepper
1 tsp. dried thyme leaves
1/2 tsp. ground red pepper (preferably cayenne)
1 1/2 C. chicken or vegetable broth
1/2 C. heavy cream

3 ¹/₂ C. cooked rice
³/₄ C. green onions, finely chopped
1 C. packed, lump crabmeat (picked over), about ¹/₂ lb.

P eel the shrimp and refrigerate shrimp until ready to use.
In a large skillet melt the butter with the oil. Add the tomato sauce, bell peppers, celery, garlic, salt, white pepper, thyme and red pepper; saute over medium heat 5 minutes, stirring frequently. Add the stock and continue cooking over high heat for 10 minutes, stirring occasionally. Stir in the cream and simmer about 4 minutes. Add the shrimp and simmer 3 minutes longer, stirring occasionally. Stir in the rice, green onions and crabmeat, keeping the lumps of crabmeat intact as much as possible. Heat through and serve immediately. Serves 6.

RED BEANS AND RICE

1 lb. red kidney beans
1 clove garlic, finely chopped
1 large onion, finely chopped
Salt and pepper to taste
1 bay leaf
1¹/₂ lb. smoked sausage
1 Tb. cooking oil

S oak beans in cold water overnight. Saute onions and chopped garlic until translucent. Add beans, and the water in which they were soaked, smoked sausage cut in 1¹/₂" pieces, bay leaf, salt and pepper, and more water to cover. Cook slowly for several hours. Serve over rice. Red beans and rice freeze well and will be even better the next day.

ORANGE RICE

1 C. rice
2 C. orange juice
Salt and pepper
¹/₂ tsp. tarragon

C ombine ingredients and bring to a boil. Cover and simmer over low heat for 20 minutes. Serve immediately.

BLACK BEANS AND YELLOW RICE

1-lb. package black beans
2/3 C. olive oil
6 cloves garlic
2 bay leaves
1 green sweet pepper, finely chopped
1½ stalks celery, finely chopped
1 Tbs. white vinegar
Salt and pepper

B ring beans and water to a boil and boil slowly for qne hour. Reduce heat and add remaining ingredients except vinegar. Cook slowly (about four hours) until beans are tender and beginning to thicken. Add vinegar and cook 10 more minutes. Salt and pepper to taste.

1 C. water
½ C. long grain white rice
½ tsp. adobo criollo seasoning
¼ tsp. turmeric
1 Tb. butter

P lace all ingredients in a saucepan with tight-fitting lid. Let cook for 20 minutes. Stir to fluff.

1 medium red onion, chopped
Oil and vinegar in cruets
Chopped cilantro if desired

T o serve: Place large mound of yellow rice on serving plates. Add generous portion of black beans on top. Sprinkle with chopped onions and cilantro and dress with oil and vinegar.

Note: If you want to save a lot of time and effort with much the same result, use canned "frijoles negroes" (black beans) and a package of Mahatma Yellow Rice.

OTHER GRAINS

DOUBLE-CHEESE POLENTA

3/4 C. chopped onion
3 Tbs. olive oil or unsalted butter
2 C. yellow cornmeal
1 1/3 C. half and half
2/3 C. plus 1/2 C. freshly grated Parmesan
2 1/3 C. grated mozzarella

In a kettle cook the onion in the oil over moderately low heat, stirring, until it is softened. Add 5 C. water, bring the liquid to a boil, and add 1 C. of the cornmeal, a little at a time, stirring constantly. Reduce heat to low, add the remaining 1 C. cornmeal in a thin stream, stirring constantly, and stir in the half and half, 2/3 C. of the parmesan, and salt to taste.

Pour half the mixture into a buttered 9" x 13" baking dish, spread it evenly, and sprinkle the top with 1/4 C. of the remaining Parmesan and half of the mozzarella. Smooth the remaining cornmeal mixture evenly over the mozzarella and sprinkle the top with the remaining 1/4 C. Parmesan and the remaining mozzarella.

Bake the polenta on the middle of a preheated 350° F. oven for 30 to 40 minutes, or until the cheese topping is melted and golden, and let it cool slightly before cutting. Serves 8.

QUINOA WITH SUN-DRIED TOMATOES

Quinoa is a Peruvian grain with a nutty flavor and makes a great alternative to rice.

1 C. quinoa
1 tsp. butter
8 sun-dried tomatoes (not oil packed), chopped
2 shallots, finely chopped
1 clove garlic, finely chopped
2 C. defatted reduced-sodium chicken broth or water
Pinch of ground red pepper (cayenne)
2 Tbs. chopped fresh parsley
Salt & freshly ground black pepper to taste

Place quinoa in a fine-meshed sieve and rinse under warm running water for 1 minute. Set aside.
    Heat butter in a heavy medium saucepan over medium heat. Add tomatoes, shallots and garlic and saut for 3 to 5 minutes or until the shallots are softened. Add chicken broth or water and bring to a boil. Stir in the quinoa and ground red pepper, return to a boil, then reduce heat to low and simmer, covered, for about 30 minutes or until the liquid has been absorbed. Let sit for 5 minutes and fluff grains with a fork to separate. Stir in parsley and season with salt and pepper. Serves 4.
Adapted from Eating Well New Favorites Cookbook

JEANNE'S GOLDEN CHEESE GRITS

4 C. water
1 C. yellow grits (substitute white if you cannot find yellow)
1/2 C. half-and -half
1/2 stick of butter
2 Tb. chopped garlic
1/2 lb. yellow cheese, grated

Boil grits in water for 25 minutes. Add, half-and-half, butter and garlic and half the cheese. Turn into oven proof dish and top with remaining cheese. Bake at 350° F. for 30 minutes.

side dishes-vegetables

VEGETABLES

REAL MASHED POTATOES

3 or 4 large baking potatoes
Salt
Milk and/or cream
Butter
White pepper

Wash and peel the potatoes, cut into lengthwise quarters, and set in a saucepan with lightly salted water to cover. Boil for 15 minutes or so, until potatoes are tender when pierced with a knife. Immediately drain and put through a ricer into a heavy bottomed saucepan. Stir with a wooden spoon over moderate heat for a minute or more until potatoes begin to film bottom of pan, indicating excess moisture has been evaporated. Beat in several Tbs. milk and/or cream to lighten them slightly, then a Tbs. butter and salt and white pepper to taste. If you are serving them immediately, beat in milk and/or cream until the potatoes are the consistency you wish, and more butter if you like.

You may cook them an hour or so ahead. In this case add only a minimum of milk and/or cream and butter and set pan in another larger pan of hot but not simmering water. Cover the potato pan only partially-hot potatoes must not be covered airtight or they develop an off taste. At serving time, uncover, raise heat, and beat the potatoes with a wooden spoon, beating in more milk and/or cream and butter to taste.

GARLIC MASHED POTATOES

1 large head of garlic
1 tsp. olive oil
2 lbs. baking potatoes, peeled and cut into 1" chunks
1½ tsp. salt
3 Tbs. unsalted butter
¼ C. low-fat milk
1 C. low-fat cottage cheese, at room temperature
A pinch of nutmeg
¼ to ½ tsp. freshly ground pepper

Preheat the oven to 350° F. With a sharp knife, cut off the top quarter of the head of garlic. Place the garlic, cut side up, on a 6" square of aluminum foil. Drizzle the olive oil over the top and wrap snugly in the foil. Bake for 1 hour. Remove and set aside to cool slightly.

In a large saucepan, combine the potatoes with 1 tsp. salt. Add water to cover and bring to a boil over high heat. Reduce the heat to moderately high and boil until fork tender, 12 to 15 minutes. Drain and return to the pan. Place the pan over high heat for about 30 seconds, shaking it once or twice to dry out the potatoes. Transfer the potatoes to a large bowl and add the butter.

In a medium saucepan, warm the milk over moderate heat, 1 to 2 minutes. Squeeze the soft garlic pulp into the milk and add the remaining ½ tsp. salt. Pour this mixture over the potatoes and mash with a hand held masher.

Add the cottage cheese, nutmeg and pepper and continue mashing until well blended and smooth. Serve hot. Serves 6.

GARLIC FRIED POTATOES

4 to 6 medium sized "boiling" or all purpose potatoes, all the
    same size and shape
Olive oil
8 to 12 large cloves of garlic, whole, unpeeled (or more, they will not
go to waste)
Salt and pepper
Large pinch of thyme, sage or rosemary

Wash and peel the potatoes, and cut into quarters lengthwise. Dry
in a clean towel. Film a medium sized heavy frying pan (non-stick
recommended) with 1/4" olive oil and heat to very hot but not smoking.
Add potatoes and let sit over moderately high heat for 2 minutes. Toss,
shaking pan by handle to make them jump and turn, and let sit 2 minutes
more. This sears the outside and helps prevent them from sticking to the
pan. Continue sauteing, tossing fairly frequently for 7 to 8 minutes more,
until the potatoes are lightly browned all over. Then add the unpeeled
garlic cloves, and toss the potatoes with a sprinkling of salt and herbs.
Cover pan and cook over moderately low heat, tossing occasionally, for 8 to
10 minutes more, until potatoes are tender. Correct seasoning.

    If not to be served immediately, keep warm but do not cover the
pan or potatoes will lose their freshly cooked taste.

    At serving time, raise heat and toss the potatoes again for a moment
or two, and serve. Each guest crushes his garlic with a fork and the soft
savory flesh oozes out to mix with the potatoes (Actually, our children, all
of whom are now twenty-something, still fight for them and squeeze them
directly into their mouths.) Serves 4-6.

ROASTED POTATOES WITH TARRAGON AIOLI SAUCE

3 lbs. thin-skinned potatoes, such as red new potatoes or small
Yukon gold potatoes. A mix of red and white creates interest.
3 Tbs. olive oil
Salt and pepper
Tarragon aioli sauce (see p. 237)

Mix washed whole potatoes with the oil in a 10" by 15" inch pan.
Lightly sprinkle with salt and pepper. Roast in 400° F. oven, shaking pan occasionally, until tender when pierced, 45 to 50 minutes (35 to 40 minutes in convection oven.) Serve hot or warm with tarragon aioli.

SWEET POTATO HOME FRIES

1$1/2$ lbs. sweet potatoes, cut into medium dice
$3/4$ lb. red potatoes, cut into medium dice
Salt
2 Tbs. butter
2 Tbs. vegetable oil
$1/2$ medium onion, minced
1 small clove garlic, minced
$1/4$ tsp. dried dill
$1/4$ tsp. caraway seeds
Ground black pepper

Bring 3 qts. water to boil in a soup kettle. Add potatoes and 1 Tb.
salt. Boil until vegetables are just tender, about 5 minutes; drain.
Heat butter and oil in a medium skillet. Add onions and garlic; saute until softened, about 2 minutes. Add the potatoes; saute until golden brown, about 4 minutes. Stir in dill and caraway seeds. Season with 1 tsp. salt and $1/4$ tsp. pepper or to taste. Serve immediately. Can be served with warm maple syrup. Serves 4-6.

YAM CASSEROLE SOUTH FLORIDA STYLE

4 yams, boiled and peeled
2 ripe oranges, sectioned
2 Tbs. brown sugar
2 Tbs. cornstarch
1/4 tsp. salt
1 C. fresh Florida orange juice
1 Tbs. sugar
1 Tbs. slivered orange rind

Peel and cut the oranges into sections, removing all seeds and membranes. Cut the yams into sections about 1" square and combine with orange sections in a shallow baking dish or casserole. In a saucepan combine the sugar, cornstarch and salt. To this gradually add the orange juice, mixing thoroughly. Bring this to a boil, stirring constantly, and boil for 1 minute. Then stir in the butter and slivered orange rind. Pour this hot mixture over the orange sections and the yams. Bake at 375° F. for 30 minutes. Serve immediately. Serves 4.

YAMS WITH LIME BUTTER

6 cooked yams
1/2 C. melted butter
2 to 3 Tbs. Key (or Persian) lime juice
1/2 tsp. salt
1/8 tsp. black pepper

Blend thoroughly the melted butter with the Key lime juice, salt and pepper. Peel the cooked yams, cut into quarters lengthwise, place in a baking dish, and pour the lime-butter sauce over them. Bake at 350° F. for about 15 minutes, basting the yams periodically with the sauce. Serve while still very hot. Serves 6.

THE BEST EVER CORN ON THE COB

Most people boil corn on the cob, but when the fresh sweet ears are available in the summer, try this:

4 ears of sweet corn on the cob, in shucks, soaked in a sink of cold water for at least 30 minutes.
Sprinkle mix:
>   1 Tb. salt
>   1 1/2 tsp. chili powder
>   1 lime, cut into wedges

Grill ears until done, about 20 minutes for 4 ears on medium hot grill. When serving, pull shucks away, rub corn with lime wedge, and sprinkle with the chili salt to taste. You may never want butter again!

CREAMED ONIONS AND MUSHROOMS WITH TARRAGON

10 oz. pearl onions, unpeeled
3 Tbs. unsalted butter
1 Tbs. all purpose flour
1 C. milk
1/2 lb. tightly closed small mushrooms, quartered
1 tsp. medium dry sherry, or to taste
1/2 tsp. fresh lemon juice
1/4 tsp. dried tarragon
2 Tbs. chopped fresh parsley

In a 1 1/2 qt. microwave-safe casserole combine the onions with 2 Tbs. water and microwave them, covered on HIGH for 2 minutes. Drain the onions in a colander, let them cool until they can be handled, and peel them. Wipe the casserole dry and microwave on HIGH 2 Tbs. butter for 1 minute, or until it's melted. Whisk in the flour and microwave on HIGH for 1 minute, and add the milk in a stream, whisking. Microwave the sauce, uncovered on HIGH for 9 minutes or until it is thickened, stirring every 3 minutes.

In a microwave-safe shallow glass dish heat the remaining 1 Tbs. butter on HIGH for 30 seconds. Stir in the mushrooms, sherry, lemon juice, salt and pepper to taste and microwave covered on HIGH for 2 minutes. Stir into the sauce the mushroom mixture, onions, parsley, salt and pepper to taste and microwave the mixture on HIGH for 1 minute or until heated through. Serves 4-6.

PORTOBELLO MUSHROOM SANDWICHES

2 Tbs. mayonnaise (low fat works fine)
2 Tbs. nonfat sour cream or plain yogurt
1 tsp. fresh lemon juice
1 Tb. olive oil
2 4-oz. portobello mushrooms, stems removed, caps wiped clean and sliced ³/₈ inch thick
Salt and freshly ground pepper to taste
8 slices sourdough bread, or two small French loaves cut in half, and half again lengthwise (to make 4 sandwiches)
1 clove garlic, halved
1 C. loosely packed basil leaves, washed, dried and torn into shreds if large.
2 vine-ripened tomatoes, cored and sliced

In a small bowl, stir together mayonnaise, sour cream or yogurt, and lemon juice. Prepare a grill or preheat the broiler. Brush olive oil over the cut sides of the mushrooms. Grill or broil the mushroom slices until tender and golden, 2 to 3 minutes per side. Season with salt and pepper. Meanwhile, toast bread on the grill or under broiler. Rub both sides of bread with garlic cloves.

Spread half of mayonnaise mixture over 4 toasted bread slices, and arrange basil on top. Top with the grilled mushroom slices, followed by tomato slices and salt and pepper to taste. Finish with a dollop of the mayonnaise and top with the remaining pieces of toast. Cut sandwiches in half and serve immediately. Serves 4.

BLACK-EYED PEAS WITH MUSHROOMS

This fabulous recipe is from Madhur Jaffrey's incomparable *Indian Cooking*.

1¼ C. dried black-eyed peas, picked over, washed and
    drained
5 C. water
½ lb. fresh mushrooms
6 Tbs. vegetable oil
1 tsp. whole cumin seeds
A 1" stick of cinnamon
1½ medium onions, peeled and chopped
4 cloves garlic, peeled and finely chopped
4 medium tomatoes, peeled and chopped
2 tsp. ground coriander seeds
1 tsp. ground cumin seeds
½ tsp. ground turmeric
¼ tsp. cayenne pepper
2 tsp. salt
Freshly ground black pepper
3 Tbs. chopped fresh coriander (or fresh parsley)

If you're from the South, this is a *must* for New Year's Day! Put the peas and water into a heavy pot and bring to a boil. Cover, reduce heat and simmer gently for 2 minutes. Turn off the heat and let the pot sit, covered and undisturbed for 1 hour.

While the pot is resting, cut the mushrooms through their stems into ⅛" slices.   Heat the oil in a frying pan over medium heat. When hot, put in the whole cumin seeds and the cinnamon stick. Let them sizzle for 5 to 6 seconds. Now put in the onions and garlic. Stir and fry until the onion pieces turn brown at the edges. Put in the mushrooms. Stir and fry until the mushrooms wilt. Now put in the tomatoes, ground coriander, ground cumin, turmeric, and cayenne. Stir and cook for a minute. Cover, turn heat to low and let this mixture cook in it's own juices for 10 minutes. Turn off the heat under the frying pan.

Bring the peas to a boil again. Cover, turn heat to low and simmer for 20 to 30 minutes or until they are tender. To this pea and water mixture, add the mushroom mixture, salt, black pepper and fresh coriander. Stir to mix and bring to a simmer. Simmer, uncovered on medium low heat for another 30 minutes. Stir occasionally. Remove cinnamon stick before serving. Serves 6.

GLAZED ROASTED SHALLOTS AND GARLIC

3 3/4 lbs. large shallots, peeled
2 lg. heads of garlic (about 32 cloves), separated into cloves
   and peeled
3/4 C. chicken stock or canned low sodium broth
2 Tbs. fresh lemon juice
2 Tbs. sugar
1 tsp. salt
1/2 tsp. freshly ground pepper
3 Tbs. unsalted butter

Preheat oven to 375° F.. Place the shallots and garlic in a single layer in a shallow baking pan. In a small nonreactive saucepan, combine the chicken stock and lemon juice and bring to a boil over high heat. Pour the hot stock over the shallots and garlic and sprinkle with the sugar, salt and pepper. Cover with aluminum foil and bake for 45 minutes. Remove the foil, stir gently and bake uncovered for 20 to 30 minutes longer until the shallots are very tender.

In a large non-stick skillet, melt 1 1/2 Tbs. of the butter over moderate heat. Add half the shallots and garlic and some of their cooking liquid. Increase the heat to moderately high and cook, shaking the pan frequently until the shallots and garlic are golden brown and caramelized all over, 5 to 7 minutes. Transfer to an oven proof serving dish. Rinse out the skillet and repeat with the remaining butter, shallots, garlic and cooking liquid. Serve hot. Serves 10-12.

The recipe can be prepared up to 1 day ahead. Let cool, cover and refrigerate. Let return to room temperature before baking in a 375° F. oven for about 10 minutes, until heated through.

Be sure to buy large firm shallots and heads of garlic; avoid any that are sprouting. Roast the shallots and garlic with a sprinkling of sugar to release their nutty sweetness. When tender and caramelized, quickly saute with butter to add the final glaze.

HOW TO COOK A FRESH ARTICHOKE

Artichokes can be cooked whole, or you may prepare just the bottoms. Both boil in a pot of "acidulated" water, meaning water with vinegar added.

Whole: With a large, sharp knife, cut off top 1/2 inch of artichoke (the pointed end). With scissors, trim the points of remaining leaves, about 1/2 inch. Rub cut edges with lemon. Simmer about 30 minutes in large pot of water to which you have added 1 Tb. vinegar. The artickokes are done when the bottom is easily pierced with a small knife.

Serve whole artichokes with drawn butter or other dipping sauce for those who like to savor the bit of flesh at the base of the leaves. Or you may cut away leaves, remove the choke, and serve just the bottoms.

Bottoms only: Before cooking, snap off all leaves. With large, sharp knife, trim off entire cone-shaped top. Using a small paring knife, trim the bright green areas left where leaves were removed, as well as stem and base. Rub all cut edges well with lemon. Cook as above in acidulated water.

After cooking, remove the choke with a spoon or melon baller.

THE ONLY REAL WAY TO COOK GREEN BEANS

Fresh green beans
Salt
Butter
Thyme, basil, tarragon or other favorite herb
Lemon juice
White pepper

Remove stems and ends from green beans. Bring a large pot of water to a boil. Add salt to water. Immerse green beans in the boiling water for 5-8 minutes. Check for tenderness by trying one. It should be "al dente," tender crisp, or however it suits you.

Drain the beans, immerse immediately in cold water to stop cooking. You can leave them in the cold water while you prepare other dishes. When you are ready to finish them, melt some butter in a saucepan, skillet or pot, add a sprinkling of your herbs of choice, a squeeze of lemon juice and white pepper. Heat until just nice and warm, bathing them in the herb butter.

Note: This is the best method for cooking fresh asparagus as well. Just snap off lower end of stems, drop the stalks in boiling water, and cook until tender. The secret is in cooling the vegetables down immediately so they will stop cooking.

GREEN BEANS WITH WALNUTS AND BROWN BUTTER

½ lb. green beans, trimmed
1 Tbs. unsalted butter
2 Tbs. finely chopped walnuts

Prepare the green beans as directed in the previous recipe. In a skillet cook the butter and the walnuts over moderate heat, swirl the skillet occasionally, until the foam subsides and the butter is nut brown. Add the beans, drained well, toss them with the butter mixture, and season them with salt and freshly ground pepper. Serves 2.

FAVORITE BROCCOLI

2 heads fresh broccoli (or 2 pkg. frozen broccoli)
3 oz. cream cheese
1 tsp. chives
1 tsp. lemon juice
slivered almonds
1 can cream of shrimp (or chicken) soup

Steam or boil broccoli and drain well. Melt soup & cream cheese. Add 1 tsp. chives and lemon juice. Pour over broccoli, sprinkle with slivered almonds. Heat and serve. Serves 4.

SPINACH PROVENCALE

2 lbs. fresh spinach (or 2 pkg. frozen chopped spinach; thaw and
squeeze to remove water)
1 lg. onion
1 clove garlic
1 C. Parmesan cheese
2 eggs, beaten
Olive oil
Salt and pepper

Saute chopped onions and garlic in olive oil. Add spinach. Cover and
cook for 2 minutes. Add eggs, $^1/_2$ C. parmesan, salt and pepper to taste,
and spinach. Pour mixture into a buttered baking dish, and sprinkle with
remaining Parmesan. Dot with butter, and bake for 10 to 15 minutes in a
375° F. oven.

CREAMED SPINACH

2 pkg. frozen chopped spinach, thawed
2 Tbs. butter
Pinch of ground nutmeg
1 Tb. cornstarch
1 C. whipping cream
Salt and white pepper

In a colander, press as much water from thawed spinach as you can. Melt
the butter in large skillet. Add spinach, sprinkle with nutmeg, salt and
white pepper. Cook over low heat until most of moisture has evaporated.

Add cornstarch and stir, then add the whipping cream and stir.
Simmer until thickened and warmed through. Adjust seasoning with salt
and white pepper.

Note: For a low-cal version of this, subsititute reduced fat chicken
broth for cream.

TOMATOES PROVENCALE

6 firm, ripe red tomatoes (about 3" in diameter)
Salt and pepper
1 to 2 cloves mashed garlic
3 Tbs. minced shallots or green onions
4 Tbs. fresh basil and parsley, or parsley only
1/8 tsp. thyme
1/4 tsp salt
Large. pinch of pepper
1/4 C. olive oil
1/2 C. fine, white, dry bread crumbs

Preheat oven to 400° F. Remove stems and cut tomatoes in half cross wise. Gently press out juice and seeds. Sprinkle the halves lightly with salt and pepper.

Blend all the ingredients (except tomatoes) in a mixing bowl. Correct seasoning. Fill each tomato half with a spoonful or two of the mixture. Sprinkle with a few drops of olive oil. Arrange the tomatoes in a shallow oiled roasting pan. Do not crowd them.

Shortly before serving, place them in the upper third of the preheated oven and bake for 10 to 15 minutes, or until tomatoes are tender but hold their shape, and the bread crumb filling has browned lightly. Serves 6.

SLOW ROASTED TOMATOES

A succulent, low calorie side dish, these can be made in summer and frozen to enjoy a taste of July in January.

Large vine-ripened tomatoes
Olive oil
Basil
Chopped garlic or garlic powder
Salt and pepper

Cut tomatoes in half sideways. Drizzle with olive oil, sprinkle on basil, garlic, salt and pepper. Roast on cooking sheet at 325° for 2-3 hours until they begin to caramelize.

RATATOUILLE

(Pron. rat-a-too-ee) An eggplant casserole from Provence.

1/2 lb. eggplant, peeled and cut into lengthwise slices 3/8 inch thick, 3 inches long, and 1 inch wide
1/2 lb. zucchini, scrubbed, sliced the same size as the eggplant
1 tsp. salt
6-7 Tbs. olive oil (more if needed)
1/2 lb. yellow onions, thinly sliced
1 C. sliced green bell peppers
2 cloves garlic, pressed
1 lb. firm ripe red tomatoes, peeled, seeded and juiced
3 Tbs. minced parsley
Salt and pepper

P lace eggplant and zucchini slices in a bowl and toss with 1 tsp. salt. Let stand for 30 minutes. Drain. Dry each slice with a towel. One layer at a time, saute the eggplant and then the zucchini in hot olive oil for about a minute on each side to brown very lightly. Remove to a side dish.

In the same skillet, cook the onions and peppers slowly in olive oil for about 10 minutes or until tender but not browned. Stir in the garlic and season to taste.

Slice the tomato pulp into 3/8 inch strips. Lay them over the onions and peppers. Season with salt and pepper. cover the skillet and cook over low heat for 5 minutes, or until tomatoes have begun to render their juice. Uncover, baste the tomatoes with the juices, raise heat and boil for several minutes, until juice has almost entirely evaporated.

Place a third of the tomato mixture in the bottom of a 2 1/2 quart stove-top safe casserole dish and sprinkle 1 Tb. parsley over it. Arrange half the eggplant and zucchini on top, then half the remaining tomatoes and parsley. Put in the rest of the eggplant and zucchini, and finish with the remianing tomatoes and parsley.

Cover the casserole and simmer over low heat for 10 minutes. Uncover, tip casserole and baste with the rendered juices. Correct seasoning if necessary. Raise heat slightly and cook uncovered for about 15 minutes more, basting several times, until juices have evaporated leaving a spoonful or two of flavored olive oil. Do not let vegetables scorch on bottom of casserole

Set aside uncovered. Can be served hot, at room temperature or cold. Serves 6-8 *Julia Child, Mastering the Art of French Cooking.*

GRILLED VEGGIES

Your choice of fresh vegetables, such as zucchini, onions, eggplant, tomatoes, mushrooms, etc., cut into slices, wedges or strips
Olive oil and herb marinade
Salt and pepper

Brush vegetables with marinade and let them soak it in for 30 minutes before grilling. Place over grill using basket designed to hold smaller items. Grill for 20-30 minutes depending on vegetable and desired doneness. Tomatoes will cook faster, so be careful not to let them "melt." Large onion chunks or slices will take longer.

Salt and pepper to taste before serving.

ROASTED PEPPERS

A basic recipe:

Your choice of red, green or yellow bell peppers or other chiles

Over a gas flame or under a broiler, roast peppers until well charred on all sides. Place them in a plastic bag and let steam for about 15 minutes. Remove and pull charred skin away. Remove the stalks from the peppers, cut off tops, cut them open, and remove seeds and veins.

At this point, peppers can be used in recipes, stored in zipper bags for upcoming use, or frozen for later use.

CONFETTI SQUASH SAUTE

1 medium onion
4 small zucchini
4 small yellow squash
1 large red pepper
1 large green pepper
1 Tb. olive oil
1/4 C. butter
1 1/2 tsp. thyme
1/2 tsp. white pepper

Slice all vegetables into julienne sticks. Place in a colander. Sprinkle with salt, and allow to drain. Pat dry. Heat oil and butter in a large skillet. Saute vegetables until crisp-tender, about 10 minutes. Sprinkle with thyme and pepper. Toss. Serves 6-8.

SQUASH WITH SOUR CREAM

2 lbs. summer squash
2 Tbs. butter or margarine
1/2 C. minced onion
1 tsp. Ac'cent (optional)*
Salt
1/2 C. sour cream
dill
paprika

Dice squash. Cook, covered, in 1/2" to 1" boiling salted water until tender, about 5 minutes, drain. Melt butter in a saucepan; add onion and cook until tender, but not brown. Add the drained squash, Ac'cent and salt and paprika to taste. Stir in sour cream; heat, but do not boil. To serve, sprinkle with dried dill and paprika. Serves 6.

* This recipe came from a time before MSG became politically incorrect.

HARVEST BAKED ACORN SQUASH

3 acorn squash
1 13¹/₂ oz. can crushed pineapple, drained
1 apple, unpeeled and diced
1 C. celery, chopped
¹/₂ C. walnuts, chopped
¹/₂ C. butter
¹/₂ C. brown sugar
¹/₂ tsp. cinnamon
¹/₂ tsp. salt

Cut squash in half so edges are scalloped; clean out seeds. Place in pan with 2" water. Bake, cut side down in a 350° F. oven for 45 minutes or until tender. Combine remaining ingredients. Spoon into squash centers after removing water. Bake, cut side up for 15 to 20 minutes.

STUFFED CHRISTOPHENE (a.k.a. chayote squash or mirliton)

3 christophenes
2 Tbs. butter
Salt and pepper
¹/₂ minced onion
1 C. buttered bread crumbs
1 C. grated cheddar cheese
Celery salt
Seasoned salt

Wash christophene, cut in half lengthwise and boil in salted water until tender. Cool. Remove seeds with a tablespoon. Scoop out flesh, keeping shells intact. Mash flesh with salt, pepper, celery salt and seasoned salt to taste. Add butter, then cheese. Add bread crumbs. Mix well and spoon back into shells. Place in a shallow baking pan and sprinkle with additional bread crumbs. Bake at 350° F. for 25 minutes.
Serves 6.
Maverick Sea Fare

VEGETABLE MEDLEY

2 or 3 zucchini
Salt and pepper
2 or 3 large. carrots
2 or more turnips
2 or 3 parsnips
2 Tbs. butter (or more)
Minced fresh green herbs such as chives, basil, chervil, and
    parsley (optional)

Cut the tips off each end of the zucchini, and scrub but don't peel
them. Slice very thin crosswise (about $1/8$"). Toss in a bowl with a good
sprinkling of salt, and let drain while preparing the other vegetables. Peel
and cut all of them into equally thin rounds.

Vegetables may be prepared several hours in advance; cover and
refrigerate.

Just before serving, heat the butter in a frying pan or wok and add
the carrots, turnips, and parsnips, tossing them almost continually over
high heat. Meanwhile, drain the zucchini and dry in paper towels. When
the other vegetables are becoming tender, add the zucchini. Toss for 2 or 3
minutes. Vegetables should retain a lightly crunchy texture. Season to
taste, toss with a little fresh butter if you wish, and the optional green
herbs. Serve at once. Serves 6-8.
Julia Child, Julia Child & Company

DR.DOG

PRESENTS

WWOBBQ

WILD WOMEN OF BAR-B-QUE

Pro Wrestling and Dinner

MEAN MAMA JAMA

SEE

TOBY WAN KENOBY

MEAN MAMA JAMA vs. TOBY WAN KENOBY
IN A WINNER GETS THE BISCUIT - STEEL VAT B-B-Q SAUCE MATCH

better than bones
-breads and pizza

BETTER THAN BONZ

BREADS AND PIZZA

COCONUT BREAD CASA MARINA

3/4 C. plus 2 Tb. sugar
1 large egg
2 Tbs. peanut or canola oil
3 Tbs. canned cream of coconut
1 C. milk
1 tsp. coconut extract
3 C. all-purpose flour
1 Tb. double-acting baking powder
1/8 tsp. salt

In a bowl with an electric mixer beat together the sugar, egg, oil, cream of coconut, milk, and coconut extract for 1 minute. Into a large bowl sift together the flour, baking powder, and salt. Stir the milk mixture into the flour mixture and pour the batter into a greased loaf pan, 9" x 5" x 3". Bake the bread in a preheated 325° F. oven for 55 minutes, or until it is pale golden around the edges. Let it cool on a rack. Makes 1 loaf.

PUMPKIN BREAD

1 16 oz. can (2 C.) pumpkin
$1/2$ C. cold water
1 C. oil
4 eggs
3 C. flour
3 C. sugar
1 tsp. baking powder
2 tsp. baking soda
1 tsp. nutmeg
Pinch of salt
1 C. raisins
1 C. nuts

Mix the first four ingredients in a blender or mix well using mixer. Sift the dry ingredients together and add the first four and mix well. Fold the raisins and nuts into the batter. Grease 3 medium loaf pans or two larger ones, taking care not to over grease. Bake at 350° F. for 1 hour.

BIG BLUEBERRY POPOVER

1 C. milk
$11/2$ tsp. vanilla extract
2 Tb. butter, melted
$1/4$ tsp. salt
$1/2$ tsp. ground nutmeg
$1/4$ C. sugar
1 C. sifted flour
2 eggs, beaten
$1/4$ tsp. ground cinnamon
1 C. blueberries

Mix first 5 ingredients plus 3 Tb. sugar in a large bowl. Stir in flour, then eggs until just combined. Let this batter stand for 5 minutes. Meanwhile, mix remaining 1 Tb. sugar and cinnamon in a separate bowl. Set aside.

Adjust oven rack to middle position and heat oven to 450° F. Place berries in a buttered 9 inch pie pan. Pour batter over the berries. Sprinkle cinnamon-sugar over the batter. Transfer pan to the oven and bake for 20 minutes. Reduce oven temperature to 350° F. Bake until popover is firm and golden brown, 15 to 20 minutes longer. Cut popover into wedges and serve immediately. Serves 6.

NUM-NUMS

Bran muffins like you've never tasted before!

2 C. bran cereal
2 C. hot water
1 C. oil
3 C. sugar
4 eggs
1 quart buttermilk
5 C. flour
2½ Tbs. baking soda
2½ Tbs. baking powder
4 C. bran cereal

Combine 2 C. bran cereal with hot water. Let stand 5 minutes. Combine oil and sugar; mix well. Add eggs and buttermilk to oil and sugar. Mix well and add soaked bran mixture. Sift in flour, soda, and baking powder. Mix thoroughly and combine with 4 C. bran cereal. Bake in well-greased muffin tins at 350° F. for 20-25 minutes.
From the White Marlin Restaurant, Aransas Pass, Texas

OATMEAL MUFFINS

1 C. oatmeal
1 C. buttermilk
1 egg, beaten
½ C. light brown sugar
1 stick butter or margarine, melted
1 C. flour

1 tsp. cinnamon
1 tsp. baking powder
1/2 tsp. baking soda
1 C. raisins, soaked in hot water for 10 minutes

Combine oats and milk. Let sit 1 hour. Add egg, sugar and butter. Mix well. Then add flour, cinnamon, baking powder and baking soda. Mix well. Add raisins. Bake at 400° F. for 20 minutes. Makes 12 muffins.

Note: You can substitute 3/4 C. applesauce for the butter for a "heart healthy" version. Also, add cut up apple, nuts or other condiments to enhance the basic muffins.

YEAST MUFFINS

1 pkg. yeast
2 C. warm water
3/4 C. melted butter or vegetable oil
4 C. self-rising flour
1 egg, beaten
1/4 C. sugar

Dissolve yeast in warm water. Mix all ingredients. Refrigerate 2 hours. Grease muffin tins and fill 2/3 full. Bake at 350° F. for 20 minutes. Batter can be covered and stored in refrigerator for future use. Makes 32 muffins.

MAMA'S ROLLS

$1\frac{1}{2}$ C. milk
$\frac{1}{2}$ C. sugar
1 Tb. salt
$\frac{1}{4}$ C. shortening
6 C. flour, sifted
1 egg
$\frac{1}{2}$ C. lukewarm water
2 pkg. yeast

Dissolve yeast in warm water and set aside. Pour the milk into a heavy saucepan, add sugar and salt. Heat to warm, then pour into a big bowl. Add shortening, followed by 3 C. of the flour. Beat with mixer. Then add egg and yeast mixture. Beat again. Add 2-3 C. more of flour until "stiff enough." (Mama's directions...)

Turn out onto a floured board and knead. Grease a big bowl with cooking oil. Put in dough and turn it over in the bowl until coated with oil. Cover bowl with plastic wrap. Let rise until double. Place on floured board, knead a little bit, then form rolls and let rise another hour. Bake in a greased pan at 350° F. about 10-15 minutes. Makes 3 dozen.

SCONES

2 C. flour
2 tsp. baking powder
1 1/2 tsp. sugar
1/2 tsp. salt
2 Tb. shortening
1 egg
1/4 to 1/2 C. milk

Mix together the dry ingredients. With fingertips, lightly rub shortening into flour mixture until it resembles coarse meal. Beat egg until it froths and set 1 Tb. aside in a small dish. Beat milk into remaining egg and pour over flour mixture. Use just enough milk to make a soft dough. Mix together until dough can be gathered into a ball.

Dust dough lightly with flour and roll out on a lightly floured surface to a thickness of 3/4 inch. Cut into triangles or 2-inch rounds. Reroll and cut scraps. Place 1 inch apart on a greased baking sheet. Brush tops lightly with reserved egg. Bake at 400° F. for 15 minutes or until light brown. Serve warm.

GERMAN STYLE KOLACHES

2 C. milk, heated
3/4 C. shortening
2 yeast cakes or 2 pkg. dry yeast
1/4 C. lukewarm water

1 Tb. sugar
2 tsp. salt
4 egg yolks
1/2 C. sugar
6 C. flour
1/2 C. melted butter

Melt shortening in hot milk; cool to lukewarm. Dissolve yeast in warm water. Sprinkle sugar over yeast in mixing bowl. Mix salt and slightly beaten egg yolks, milk and shortening mixture, and 1/2 C. sugar in a small bowl. Add to the yeast, which by this time should be at the foamy stage. Place liquid and yeast in large bowl; add flour a little at a time until all is used. Work dough with hands until it is glossy. Cover and let rise until double in bulk, about 1 hour.

Preheat oven to 425° F. After dough has risen, drop by the tablespoon on a floured board and roll into a ball. Place onto a greased baking sheet about an inch apart. Brush each round with melted butter. Let rise until light, about 30 minutes.

Make an indentation on the top with a thumb and put about 1-2 tsp. fruit or other filling in it. Sprinkle with butter crumb topping and bake about 15 minutes at 425° F. Makes about 4 dozen.

Butter crumb topping

Mix together 1/4 C. flour, 1/2 C. sugar, and 1 Tb. butter.

Cherry filling

Blend together 1 can cherry pie filling, 1/2 tsp. almond extract, and 1/2 tsp. butter flavoring.

Apple filling

Blend together 1 can apple pie filling, 1/2 tsp. cinnamon, 1/2 tsp. vanilla, 1/4 tsp. butter flavoring.

TOMATO BASIL BISCUITS

1 C. unbleached all-purpose flour
Pinch of sugar
1/4 tsp. salt
2 tsp. baking powder
4 Tb. unsalted butter, cold
1/4 C. half-and-half

¹/₂ C. ripe tomatoes, peeled, seeded, and coarsely chopped
¹/₃ C. basil, chopped

Preheat oven to 425° F. In a large bowl, sift together the flour, sugar, salt and baking powder. Cut the butter into ¹/₂ inch cubes and with 2 knives or a pastry blender work them into the flour until the mixture resembles coarse crumbs.

Add half and half and the tomatoes, and stir to combine thoroughly. Stir in the chopped basil. Transfer the dough to a lightly floured board and knead for 30 seconds. Pat dough to 1 inch thick and cut into 2 inch rounds. Place on baking sheet and bake about 15 minutes.

JALAPENO CORNBREAD

3 C. cornbread mix
2¹/₂ C. milk
¹/₂ C. salad oil
3 beaten eggs
1 large grated onion
3 Tb. sugar
1 C. canned cream style corn
¹/₂ C. pickled jalapeno peppers, chopped very fine
1¹/₂ C. grated yellow cheese
2 oz. chopped crisp bacon
¹/₂ C. finely chopped pimiento peppers
Fresh mashed garlic or garlic powder to suit your taste

Mix all well and bake (preferably in a large cast iron skillet) at 400°F. until done and brown.

CUSTARD CRUST CORN BREAD

1¹/₂ C. yellow cornmeal
¹/₂ C. sugar
¹/₂ C. all-purpose flour
2 tsp. salt

1 C. buttermilk
1/2 tsp. baking soda
2 large eggs, beaten
2 C. milk
2 Tbs. butter, melted

Preheat over to 350°. Lightly grease a large cast-iron skillet or other ovenproof skillet.

In a large bowl, mix the cornmeal, sugar, flour, and salt. Add the buttermilk and baking soda and mix well. Add the eggs, the regular milk, and the melted butter to the batter and mix well.

Pour the batter into the prepared skillet and bake until firm, about 45 minutes. Cut the cornbread into wedges and serve hot or at room temperature. Makes 6-8 servings.

PITA BREAD

1 package dry yeast
1 tsp. honey
1 1/2 C. warm water
3/4 tsp. salt
3 Tbs. olive oil
1 1/2 C. whole-wheat flour
1 1/2 to 2 C. bread flour

In a large mixing bowl, stir together the yeast, honey, and water. Add the salt and oil. Add the whole wheat flour, stirring vigorously for 3 minutes. Gradually add and stir in enough white flour to make a soft dough that pulls away from the side of the bowl.

Knead the dough on a lightly floured work surface for 5 to 10 minutes, or until it is smooth and elastic, using only enough additional flour to keep the dough from sticking. Place the dough back in the bowl, cover it, and let it rest in a warm place for 1 hour, or until it has doubled in size.

Preheat the oven to at least 500° F, with a pizza stone or oiled baking sheet on the lowest rack. Punch down the dough and cut it into eight pieces. Shape each into a smooth, round ball with no creases and cover again.

Flatten two balls into disks, then roll them out with a rolling pin until each is ⅛ to ¼ inch thick, keeping the other pieces of dough covered. Using a cornmeal-covered peel or spatula, slide the two pitas onto the pizza stone or baking sheet and bake for 5 minutes. Don't open the oven door during baking. Place the baked pitas into a paper bag to keep them soft while they cool. Repeat these steps until all eight pitas have been baked.

Store cooled pitas in a plastic bag at room temperature or freeze them for longer storage. Makes 8 pitas.

CREPES

3 large eggs, broken in a 4 cup measure or bowl
⅔ C. milk
⅔ C. water, plus droplets more if needed
¼ tsp. salt
3 Tb. dark sesame oil or fresh peanut oil
1 C. Wondra® or Shake 'n Blend® flour
A little peanut oil for greasing crepe pans
24 wax paper squares, 6 inches to a side

Beat the eggs to blend whites and yolks, then beat in the liquids, salt and oil; gradually beat in the flour. Let stand 20-30 minutes (or longer, if need be, in the refrigerator.)

Stir batter to be sure it is smooth, then pour 2 Tbs. into a big spoon or ladle. Take note of how full it should be for each crepe. Set a dish to hold cooked crepes and wax paper close at hand. Place crepe pan or small flat skillet over moderately high heat and brush lightly with oil (usually necessary only for the first crepe.) Flick a few droplets of water into the pan; they should sizzle. Pour a small spoonful of the batter as a test: it should sizzle, form little bubbles in the surface, and brown.

Now put sufficient batter into your big spoon or ladle for one crepe. Pour batter into center of hot pan. Immediately tip pan rapidly around to spread batter all over bottom surface. Set directly on burner, and bubbles will appear almost immediately. Let cook about 30 seconds or until an edge when lifted is brown underneath. When you shake the pan hard, the crepe will usually come loose. Flip crepe over onto its other side, either by tossing it in the air or by turning it with a spatula. Cook 15-20 seconds more. This side will brown only in spots, and is considered the underside that is never exposed to view.

Place a wax paper square on the plate, slide the crepe onto it, and cover with another square of paper to prevent the crepes from sticking. It may take some practice to get really good-looking crepes. They should not be more than 1/16 inch thick, light and delicate in texture, yet sturdy enough to be rolled around fillings. Makes 20.

Crepes can be made ahead, covered and refrigerated for 2 days or so. Or you may freeze them. Separate into smaller amounts, like 4 or 6 to a package, and wrap airtight in foil. To thaw, place in a covered dish in a 300° F. oven for 10 minutes or so until warmed through enough that you can separate them easily.

Fill crepes with anything from creamy concoctions made with such things as chopped hard-boiled eggs, herbs and cheeses or a veloute of lobster, crab or shrimp. Or go the fruity route with cherry or apple pie filling, or other favorite.

PIZZAS

BASIC PIZZA DOUGH

1 tsp. active dry yeast
1 2/3 - 2 C. unbleached or all-purpose white flour
1 C. cake flour
1 tsp. salt

In a measuring cup or small bowl, sprinkle yeast over 1/4 C. warm water; stir until dissolved. In a mixing bowl, combine 1 2/3 C. of the un-bleached or alll-purpose flour, cake flour and salt. Make a well in the center of the flour mixture and pour in the yeast mixture. With a wooden spoon, gradually stir in the flour, adding 3/4 C. warm water as you mix. Turn the dough out onto a lightly floured surface and knead until very smooth, soft and no longer sticky, about 10 minutes, adding flour as needed to keep the dought from sticking. (The dough should still be quite wet, however.)

Set the dough in an oiled bowl an dturn to coat lightly. cover with plastic wrap and let rise until doubled, 2 to 2 1/2 hours.

About 10 minutes before baking pizza, turn the dough onto the floured board, punch it down and knead briefly. Use a pastry cutter or a thin, sharp knife to divide the dough in half. (If you pull the dough apart, you risk tearing the gluten strands.) Pat each half into a ball and flatten into a disk. It is now ready to use in your favorite pizza recipe. Make enough for two 12-inch pizzas.

Below are three favorite pizza recipes which use this dough and any favorite tomato sauce, such as Paul Newman's if you don't want to make your own.

PIZZA MARGHERITA

Said to have been a favorite of Margaret of Savoy. The garlic was said to have been left out to protect the purity of her queenly breath.

$^3/_4$ lb. pizza dough
Semolina or corn meal for dusting
1 Tb. extra-virgin olive oil
$^1/_2$ C. tomato or pizza sauce
2 oz. mozzarella cheese, sliced $^1/_8$ inch thick
Salt and freshly ground black pepper to taste
$^1/_2$ C. loosely packed fresh basil leaves (1 small bunch) thoroughly rinsed.
$^1/_4$ C. freshly grated Parmesan cheese

Place a pizza stone, baking tiles or an inverted baking sheet on the bottom or lowest rack of a cold oven. Preheat for 30 minutes to 500° F.

Place dough on a lightly floured surface and pat into a disk. Use a rolling pin or your hands to roll or stretch the dough into a circle that is $^1/_4$ inch thick and 11 to 12 inches in diameter. Transfer to a semolina or cornmeal-dusted pizza peel or inverted baking sheet.

Brush the dough with a little of the olive oil to the edge. Spread tomato sauce over the dough to within $^1/_2$ inch of the edge. Distribute mozzarella slices over the tomato sauce and season with salt and pepper. Arrange basil leaves over the mozzarella, reserving a few for garnish if you wish. Sprinkle with Parmesan. Drizzle with the remaining olive oil. Carefully slide the pizza onto the heated pizza stone and bake for 6 to 8 minutes, or until the bottom is crisp and browned and the top is bubbling. Garnish with reserved basil leaves if desired. Makes one 12-inch pizza.

PIZZA ALLA SICILIANA

3/4 lb. pizza dough
Semolina or corneal for dusting
1 Tb. extra virgin olive oil
1/2 C. tomato sauce
6 black olives, pitted and sliced
6 green olives, pitted and sliced
(Go for Sicilian olives if you can find them)
3 anchovy fillets, rinsed, patted dry and chopped
1 Tb. drained capers
1 Tb. freshly grated Parmesan cheese

Place a pizza stone, baking tiles or an inverted baking sheet on the lowest rack of a cold oven; preheat for 30 minutes to 500°F.

Place dough on a lightly floured surface and pat into a disk. Use a rolling pin or your hands to roll or stretch the dough into a circle that is 1/4 inch thick and 11 to 12 inches in diameter. Transfer to a semolina or cornmeal-dusted pizza peel or inverted baking sheet.

Brush the dough with a little of the olive oil to the edge. Spread tomato sauce over the dough to within 1/2 inch of the edge. Distribute olives, anchovies and capers over the sauce. Sprinkle with cheese. Drizzle with the remaining olive oil.

Carefully slide the pizza onto the heated pizza stone and bake for 6 to 8 minutes, or until the bottom is crisp and browned and the top is bubbling. Makes one 12-inch pizza.

FOUR SEASONS PIZZA

3/4 lb. pizza dough
Semolina or cornmeal for dusting
1 Tb. extra virgin olive oil
1/2 C. tomato sauce
1 can marinated artichoke hearts
1/2 lb. mushrooms, thinly sliced
1 C. thin strips sliced coppa or salami
2 C. mozzarella or jack cheese

Place a pizza stone, baking tiles or an inverted baking sheet on the lowest rack of a cold oven; preheat for 30 minutes to 450°F.

Place dough on a lightly floured surface and pat into a disk. Use a rolling pin or your hands to roll or stretch the dough into a circle that is $1/4$ inch thick and 11 to 12 inches in diameter. Transfer to a semolina or cornmeal-dusted pizza peel or inverted baking sheet.

Brush the dough with a little of the olive oil to the edge. Spread tomato sauce over the dough to within $1/2$ inch of the edge. Mark pizza dough into four quadrants. Arrange artichokes over one section, mushrooms on another. Cover third section with sausage, and the fourth with cheese. Brush the artichokes with olive oil.

Carefully slide the pizza onto the heated pizza stone and bake for 15 to 20 minutes, or until the crust is well browned. Makes one 12-inch pizza.

dr. dog & toby

a brunch munch

A BRUNCH MUNCH

SOUR CREAM AND BREAD CRUMB FLAPJACKS

1 C. toasted fresh non-sweet white bread crumbs
4 Tb. melted butter
1 egg
$^1/_2$ C. Wondra or instant-blending flour
$^1/_2$ C. sour cream
$^1/_2$ C. or more milk
$^1/_2$ tsp. double-acting baking powder
Salt and pepper

To make toasted bread crumbs, crumb fresh bread in a blender or a processor, then spread out in a roasting pan in a preheated 350° F. oven. Toss as they cook, until they are lightly browned, 15-20 minutes, then toss in a frying pan with the melted butter over moderate heat.

Blend egg, flour, sour cream, $^1/_2$ C. milk, and baking powder in a 4 cup measure; fold in the buttered crumbs and salt and pepper to taste. Stir in driblets more milk if you think necessary.

Drop batter onto a buttered hot skillet and cook pancakes, turning when bubbles appear on the surface. Serve with melted butter and maple syrup or honey.

Julia Child, *Julia Child & Company*

BANANA PANCAKES

¹/₄ C. flour
¹/₂ tsp. baking powder
1 Tb. cinnamon
2 egg yolks, beaten
¹/₄ C. milk
1 Tb. vanilla extract
4 ripe bananas, mashed
2 Tb. butter, melted
2 egg whites, stiffly beaten
Butter or margarine for griddle
Confectioner's sugar (optional)

Sift together flour, baking powder and cinnamon. In a separate bowl, combine egg yolks, milk, and vanilla extract. Pour into dry ingredients and stir well. Stir in bananas and butter. Fold in egg whites and blend gently. Let batter settle for a few minutes.

Drop batter, 2 Tb. at a time, on a hot, buttered griddle and cook until golden brown on each side. Or, if you prefer, divide batter into 4 portions and make 4 large pancakes. For an added touch, sprinkle with confectioner's sugar. Serves 4.

PUMPKIN PANCAKES

1 C. flour
¹/₂ tsp. baking powder
4 Tb. sugar (or to taste)
1 tsp. salt
1 tsp. cinnamon
2 eggs, lightly beaten
2 C. milk
1 tsp. vanilla extract
2 lbs. pumpkin, mashed or pureed (canned will do)
Corn oil for frying

ift together flour, baking powder, sugar, salt, and cinnamon. In a separate bowl, combine eggs, milk, and vanilla. Pour into dry ingredients. Stir in pumpkin and blend well. Heat corn oil in a heavy skillet or griddle. Drop batter, 2 Tb. at a time, into skillet. Cook until golden brown on each side. Drain on paper towel. Serves 4.

MAVERICK FRENCH TOAST

French toast simply doesn't get any better!

8 slices bread (I prefer thick sliced French, soaked overnight)
4 eggs
1 C. evaporated milk
2 Tb. rum
1 Tb. sugar
1/4 tsp. salt
1/2 tsp. cinnamon
1/4 tsp. nutmeg

lace the bread slices in a pan. Mix all other ingredients together and pour over the bread to coat evenly. Let bread soak at least 1/2 hour, overnight is okay. Saute in hot butter until golden. Serve with two jugs of syrup--one straight, the other laced with rum. Yum!

This can be made up and frozen, then thawed before cooking. A great way for planning ahead for a large brunch.
Dee Carstarphen, Maverick Sea Fare

EGGS BENEDICT

This classic favorite is an open-faced sandwich of sorts, with ham or Canadian bacon and a poached egg stacked on a toasted English muffin and topped with Hollandaise sauce. (See p. 20 for instructions on poaching eggs, and p. 237 for making Hollandaise.)

Recently, Dr. Dog created these new versions that are bound to have you salivating!

HUEVOS BENEDICTOS MEXICANO

1 large tomato, sliced in 4 half inch thick slices
1 tsp. adobo criollo
1 C. refried black beans
1 Tb. olive oil
1 avocado, halved, peeled and thinly sliced
4 poached eggs
2 English muffins, split
1¼ C. "chipotlenaise" (recipe follows)
4 sprigs cilantro for garnish

Brush tomato slices with olive oil, season with adobo criollo and broil until quite brown.

Under a broiler, toast English muffins cut side down for 2 minutes. Turn, brush with remaining olive oil and toast until lightly browned.

Spread each muffin half with ¼ cup of black beans, top with broiled tomato slice, then ¼ of the sliced avocado. Place poached egg on avocado and divide "chipotlenaise" evenly over the four halves. Garnish with a sprig of cilantro. Serves 2.

CHIPOTLENAISE

3 egg yolks
1 stick butter, melted
2 Tbs. chipotle hot sauce

In a blender, combine the chipotle hot sauce and three egg yolks. Blend briefly, then add the melted butter in a slow steady stream and blend until thickened.

EGGS HENRI IV

4 1/2 inch thick filet steaks (about 2 ounces each), lightly
salted and peppered
1 Tb. olive oil
1/2 Tb. butter
1/4 C. red wine
1/4 C. beef bouillon
1 6-oz. jar marinated artichoke hearts, sliced
4 poached eggs
2 English muffins, split
1 1/4 C. bearnaise sauce (recipe follows)
4 sprigs parsley for garnish

Warm artichokes slices in their liquid. Heat butter and oil over high
heat in a heavy skillet. When butter foam begins to subside, add
steaks and saute two minutes each side for medium rare.

Remove steaks, deglaze pan with wine and bouillon, and continue to
boil until liquid reduces to about 1/3 cup.

Under a broiler, toast English muffins cut side down for 2 minutes.
Turn, brush with olive oil and toast until lightly browned.

Place a steak on each muffin half, divide sauce from skillet over the
steaks. Top with 1/4 of the sliced artichokes. Place poached egg on artichokes and divide bearnaise sauce evenly over the four halves. Garnish
with a sprig of parsley. Serves 2.

BEARNAISE SAUCE

3 egg yolks
1 stick butter, melted
1/4 C. wine vinegar
1/4 C.dry white wine or vermouth
1 Tb.minced green onion
1/2 Tb.dried tarragon
Salt and pepper

Combine the wine, vinegar, onion, tarragon and salt and pepper to taste
and microwave or boil until reduced to 2 tablespoons.

In a blender, combine the wine, vinegar mixture and three egg
yolks. Blend briefly, then add the melted butter in a slow steady stream
and blend until thickened.

EGGS PROVENCALE

4 1/2 inch thick slices of eggplant
1/4 C. olive oil
1 zucchini, thinly sliced crosswise
1 large onion, thinly sliced
1 small green pepper, sliced crosswise
1 C. canned diced tomatoes with Italian seasoning
4 poached eggs
2 English muffins, split
1 1/4 C. basil hollandaise (recipe follows)
4 caper berries for garnish

Brush eggplant with olive oil and saute in remaining olive oil until cooked through. Remove eggplant and saute zucchini, onion and green pepper until tender. Add tomatoes and boil until most of the liquid has evaporated. Salt and pepper to taste.

Under a broiler, toast English muffins cut side down for 2 minutes. Turn, brush with olive oil and toast until lightly browned.

Top each muffin half with an eggplant slice, followed by 1/4 of the sauteed vegetable mixture. Place poached egg on top and divide the basil hollandaise evenly over the four halves. Garnish with a caper berry. Serves 2.

BASIL HOLLANDAISE

3 egg yolks
1 stick butter, melted
2 Tbs. lemon juice
1 Tb. olive anchovy paste
1/2 C. minced fresh basil
Salt and pepper to taste

In a blender, combine the lemon juice, olive anchovy paste, basil and three egg yolks. Blend briefly, then add the melted butter in a slow steady stream and blend until thickened.

EGGS MANGO CARRIBBEAN

1/2 C. Major Grey mango chutney
1 large mango, peeled and sliced
4 poached eggs
2 English Muffins, split
1 1/4 C. orange rum hollandaise (recipe follows)
4 slices kiwi fruit for garnish

Under a broiler, toast English muffins cut side down for 2 minutes. Turn, brush with butter and toast until lightly browned.

Spread each muffin half with 1/4 of the mango chutney, top with 1/4 of the mango slices. Place poached egg on mango and divide orange rum hollandaise evenly over the four halves. Garnish with a slice of kiwi.

ORANGE RUM HOLLANDAISE

3 egg yolks
1 stick butter, melted
1/4 Tb. triple sec
1 1/4 Tb. Myers rum
1 Tb. orange juice
2 tsp. grated orange zest

In a blender, combine the triple sec, rum, orange juice, orange zest and three egg yolks. Blend briefly, then add the melted butter in a slow steady stream and blend until thickened.

EGGS BUBBA-DICT

Dr. Dog's redneck friends love this one!

4 muffin size slices of country ham
1/4 C. port (or white lightnin' if you have it)
2 C. cooked grits
4 poached eggs
2 English muffins, split
1 1/4 C. red eye hollandaise (recipe follows)
4 toothpicks for garnish

Fry ham slices in a little water until browned. Put aside. Deglaze skillet with wine, scraping up the ham particles. Reduce liquid to about two tablespoons. Reserve.

Under a broiler, toast Bay English Muffin cut side down for 2 minutes. Turn, brush with butter and toast until lightly browned.

Top each muffin half with a slice of ham and a serving of grits. Place poached egg on the grits and divide red eye hollandaise evenly over the four halves. Garnish with a toothpick. Serves 2.

RED EYE HOLLANDAISE
3 egg yolks
1 stick butter, melted
2 Tbs. reserved liquid from the ham

In a blender, combine the ham liquid and three egg yolks. Blend briefly, then add the melted butter in a slow steady stream and blend until thickened.

EGG BURRITOS

Scrambled eggs enclosed in egg tortillas--a favorite of that ol' egg-suckin' dawg!

12 eggs
Salt, freshly ground pepper, and hot pepper sauce
1 to 2 Tbs. butter
1/2 C. cottage cheese
1/4 C. chopped fresh parsley
1/4 tsp. fresh or dried thyme
2 C. fine tomato sauce
1/4 C. grated Cheddar cheese
Wax paper cut into 6 inch squares

Whisk eggs in a bowl with salt, pepper and hot pepper sauce to taste. Set a small non-stick frying pan over moderately high heat and brush lightly with butter. Pour in 1 1/2 Tb. of egg and tilt the pan in all directions to film the bottom. Cover the pan for a few seconds until the egg has set, then lide it out onto wax paper. You have created a crepe-like "tortilla." Repeat, making 8 in all.

Add butter to pan, and following instructions on p. 20 , scramble the remaining egg mixture. Blend with the cottage cheese and herbs and adjust seasoning.

Roll up a portion of scrambled eggs in each burrito skin. Pour the tomato sauce into a lightly buttered baking dish and arrange the burritos on top. Sprinkle on grated cheese. At this point, you may cover and refrigerate if you wish to serve at a later time.

Preheat oven to 450°F. Shortly before serving, bake in the upper third level of oven until the sauce bubbles and the cheese has melted. Do not overheat! Serves 8. *Julia Child, The Way to Cook*

KAREN'S SPANISH FRITTATA

2 Tb. olive oil or vegetable oil
1 large onion, chopped
2 medium boiled potatoes, cubed
1 Tb. butter
2 tsp. chopped garlic
6-8 large eggs
Salt and pepper to taste
Your choice of additional ingredients, such as:
      Chopped ham
      Chopped chicken
      Dry chili peppers, sauteed to soften
      Spinach and cottage cheese
      Cheese (the stronger the better)
      Green/red bell pepper chopped
      Shrimp

Saute onion in the oil on high until it turns glassy. Add potatos and butter. When onions and potatoes are slightly browning, add chopped garlic and saute a little longer. Remove skillet from heat, and turn down heat to lowest temperature on the range.

    Whisk eggs until blended in a large bowl. Add saute mix to the egg mix and combine. Add salt and pepper. (It may require a fair amount of salt because the eggs and potatoes are so bland.)

    Pur the mixture into the skillet and let it cook through on low heat, about 10 minutes. To cook the top, you can either flip the tortilla, which is messy, or set skillet under a grill with high heat until the top is sealed and browning. Serves 6.

BREAKFAST TACOS

A San Antonio tradition!

Soft flour tortillas
Scrambled eggs
Hash browned potatoes, cooked
Diced ham or sausage, cooked

Refried beans
Grated Cheddar cheese
Chopped green onions
Chopped avocados drenched in lemon juice
Carne Guisada (see recipe below)
Picante sauce

Wrap tortillas in foil and warm in oven while preparing fillings. When ready to serve, place a tortilla on a plate, top with whatever floats your boat, and roll it up.

CARNE GUISADA

1 lb. beef stew meat, cut in $1/2$ inch dice
1 large onion, chopped
2 medium potatoes, diced
Goya adobo criollo
1 bell pepper, chopped
1 C. beef stock
1 Tb. cornstarch or flour (optional)

Saute the meat in a little oil until browned on all sides. Season with adobo criollo, add onion and bell pepper and continue to saute until onions become translucent. Add potatoes and beef stock and simmer slowly until meat is tender and stew is thickened. If not thick enough, mix a Tb. of cornstarch or flour with a Tb. of water and stir into stew. Adjust seasoning with salt and pepper.

QUICK AND EASY HUEVOS RANCHEROS

1 $14^1/2$ oz. can Mexican style tomato sauce
4 eggs

There are several ways to prepare Huevos Rancheros. Some prefer to pour the sauce into a stove-top safe casserole, heat and poach the eggs directly in the sauce.
Others fry the eggs first and top with heated sauce. Serve with toast or tortillas. Serves 2-4.

FULL ENGLISH BREAKFAST

Not for the faint of heart, this cholesterol-laden breakfast is served throughout the U.K.

Eggs, any style, at least two per person
Bangers (small finger-sized sausages)
Bacon (a thicker, fatter variety than American bacon)
Sauteed mushrooms
Broiled tomato halves
Pork 'n beans
Home fried potatoes
Toast (usually cold, swiped with butter) and marmalade
Muffins, scones, or crumpets
Juices
Coffee and tea

Although it sounds heavy, when Dr. Dog is traveling abroad, he finds this breakfast particularly energizing. Serve as a buffet on a hunt table or pass family-style for a hearty winter brunch.

REWARDS

DESSERTS

SOCK-IT-TO-ME-CAKE

1 stick margarine
1 box Duncan Hines Yellow Butter Cake Mix
1 C. sour cream
3/4 C. cooking oil
1/2 C. sugar
4 eggs
3 Tbs. brown sugar
1 Tb. cinnamon

Drizzle:
1/2 C. sugar
1/4 C. buttermilk
1/4 tsp. soda
2 Tb. Karo syrup
1/2 tsp. vanilla

Empty cake mix into a bowl. Add sugar, sour cream and cooking oil. Pour in melted (but cooled) margarine. Add the eggs one at a time, beating after each addition. Pour half of the mixture in a Bundt pan. Sprinkle brown sugar and cinnamon over, Pour second half of mix on top of first half. Bake at 350°F. for 45 minutes.

Remove from oven and allow to cool. While cooling, mix the drizzle ingredients and boil slowly until slightly syrupy. Remove cake from Bundt pan and pour drizzle evenly over the top of the cake. Pierce top of cake to allow drizzle to soak in.

COFFEE CAKE

1 stick margarine
1 C. sugar
2 eggs
2 C. flour
1 tsp. baking powder
1 tsp. baking soda
1/2 tsp. salt
1 C. sour cream
1 tsp. vanilla

Cream margarine and sugar. Add eggs one at a time, beating well. Sift dry ingredients and add to creamed mixture alternately with sour cream - beginning and ending with flour mixture. Stir in vanilla.

Pour half of batter into pan (sprinkle batter with half of topping). Over topping pour remainder of batter and sprinkle rest of topping. Bake in a well-greased Bundt pan or tube pan at 350°F. for 40 minutes. Test with toothpick. It is done when toothpick comes out clean.

Topping:
1/3 C. packed brown sugar
1/4 C. sugar
1 1/4 tsp. cinnamon
3/4 C. chopped walnuts

HEATH BAR COFFEE CAKE

2 C. brown sugar
2 C. flour
1/2 lb. margarine
1 C. milk
1 tsp. soda
1 egg, well-beaten
1 tsp. vanilla
3/4 C. pecans
6 Heath bars, broken into small pieces

ix sugar, flour and margarine as you would for a pie crust, combining with knives or pastry blender until crumbly in texture. Add milk, baking soda, egg and vanilla. Mix well. Pour into greased 10" x 4" pan. Top with nuts and broken Heath bars. Bake at 350°F. for 40-45 minutes.

FRESH BLUEBERRY COFFEE CAKE

1¼ C. fresh or frozen blueberries
⅓ C. sugar
2 Tbs. cornstarch
½ C. margarine, softened
1 C. sugar
2 eggs
2 C. flour
1 tsp. baking powder
1 tsp. soda
1/2 tsp. salt
8 oz. sour cream
¾ tsp. almond extract
½ C. pecans, finely chopped

Combine blueberries, ⅓ C. sugar and cornstarch in small pan; cook over medium heat until sauce thickens, stirring constantly. Set aside.

Cream margarine, Gradually add 1 C. sugar. Add eggs one at a time. Combine flour, baking powder, soda and salt; add to creamed mixture alternately with sour cream, beginning and ending with flour mixture, Stir in almond extract.

Spoon ½ of batter into a greased 10" Bundt or tube pan. Spoon ½ of the blueberry sauce into pan, swirling partially through batter with knife. Repeat with remaining batter and sauce. Sprinkle with pecans. Bake at 350°F. for 50 minutes or until done. Let stand five minutes before removing. Invert onto serving platter and drizzle with glaze.

Glaze
¾ C. sifted powdered sugar
1 T. warm water
½ tsp. almond extract

Combine all ingredients, stirring well.

POUND CAKE

¹/₂ lb. butter
¹/₂ C. shortening
3 C. extra fine granulated sugar
3 C. cake flour
¹/₄ tsp. baking powder
1¹/₂ C. milk
5 eggs (room temperature)
1 tsp. vanilla extract

Preheat oven to 300° F. Grease and flour tube pan. Sift together cake flour and baking powder; set aside. In large mixing bowl, cream butter and shortening; add sugar, gradually, beating until light and fluffy. Mix dry ingredients, alternately with milk, into creamed mixture, beginning and ending with flour, mixing well after each addition. Add eggs, one at a time. Add vanilla extract. Pour into tube pan. Bake for 1 hour and 25 minutes. Note: DON'T PEEK AT BAKING CAKE THROUGH OPEN OVEN DOOR! Cool cake in pan for 10 minutes. Cool completely on wire rack. (For chocolate pound cake, add 3 Tbs. cocoa to dry ingredients.)

DEVIL'S FOOD POUND CAKE

1 pkg. Duncan Hines Moist Deluxe Devil's Food Cake Mix
1 6 oz. pkg. chocolate instant pudding
4 eggs
1¹/₄ C. waer
¹/₂ C. shortening or vegetable oil
12 oz. pkg. chocolate chips

Preheat oven to 350° F. Grease and flour 10" Bundt pan or tube pan. Combine cake mix, pudding mix, eggs, water, and oil in a large bowl. Beat at medium speed with electric mixer for 3 minutes. Pour into pan. Bake for 50-60 minutes, or until toothpick inserted in center comes out clean.

Cool in pan 25 minutes. Invert onto serving plate and cool completely, then add topping.

Topping:

1 6oz. pkg. semisweet chocolate chips
1/2 C. whipping cream
Combine in a small saucepan over medium heat, stirring just until morsels are melted. Cool 15 minutes, drizzle over cake.

EDGIE'S CAKE

1 C. shortening
2 1/2 C. sugar
2 eggs
2 1/2 C. flour
1/2 C. cocoa
1 C. buttermilk
2 tsp. baking soda
1 C. hot water
Pinch of salt
2 tsp. vanilla

Cream shortening and sugar. Add eggs, mix well. Sift flour and cocoa together. Add 4 tsp. to egg mixture, then alternate with milk, but last addition should be flour. Add soda to water and beat hard (the soda and water, not the whole mixture.) Add salt and vanilla. Beat all ingredients well.

Rinse a 13"x9" baking pan and shake excess water. (No greasing and flouring for this recipe.) Bake in 350° F. oven about 1 hour.

Icing:

2 C. powdered sugar
3 Tbs. cocoa
6 Tbs. melted butter or margarine
1 tsp. vanilla
Hot coffee

Mix sugar, cocoa, butter and vanilla, then add hot coffee until the sugar melts and the icing becomes spreadable. Ice the cake in the pan. This has never been a very pretty cake, but its deep chocolaty richness has made it a family favorite.

MISSISSIPPI MUD CAKE

Another version for chocolate lovers:
2 sticks margarine
2 C. sugar
1½ C. all-purpose flour
4 eggs
3 T. cocoa
1 tsp. vanilla
1½ C. pecans
1 jar marshmallow cream

Cream sugar, butter, cocoa, eggs and vanilla. Mix well until sugar dissolves. Add flour. Beat 2-3 minutes with electric mixer. Add nuts and pour into 13" x 9" greased and floured pan. Bake in 350° F. oven for 35-40 minutes.

Remove from oven and spread with marshmallow cream while hot. Cool at least 2 hours before icing cake, overnight is better.

Icing:

4 T. cocoa
⅓ C. milk
1 stick butter
1 box powdered sugar
1 tsp. vanilla

Bring cocoa, milk and butter to a boil in a saucepan. Place sugar and vanilla in a large bowl, and pour hot mixture over. Beat until smooth, then pour over the layer of marshmallow cream.

NANCY'S NEW YORK CHEESE CAKE

Zwieback crackers (in baby food dept.)
¼ C. sugar
¼ C. butter (melted)
1½ lb. cream cheese (3 - 8oz. pkgs)
1½ C. sugar

1^{1}/$_{2}$ tsp. vanilla
1^{1}/$_{2}$ pints sour cream

P lace one layer of Zwieback crackers in cheese cake pan, crush. Combine with sugar and butter and press onto bottom and sides of cake pan.

Mix cream cheese and eggs slowly with electric mixer, adding one egg at a time. Blend in sugar and then other ingredients. Pour into crust, bake at 375°F. for 1 hour. Turn oven off, open door and leave cake in oven for 1 more hour. Refrigerate for two days to develop best flavor.

BLUEBERRY CHEESECAKE

Pie Crust:
2 C. graham cracker crumbs
^{1}/$_{4}$ lb. melted butter
2 Tbs. sugar
Mix well before lining and pack. Preheat oven to 350 degrees. Bake in a 9" pie pan for 6 minutes.
Filling:
2 Tbs. sugar
1 lb. cream cheese
^{1}/$_{2}$ C. sour cream
1 can Comstock blueberries

B lend cream cheese, sour cream and sugar until smooth. Pour into pie crust and top with blueberries; sprinkle top of berries with sugar and bake 5 minutes at 350° F. Chill and serve. Serves 8.

BLIND PIG CHEESECAKE

So easy a blind pig can make it.

1 C. packaged graham crackers
1/4 C. softened butter
4 3oz. pkgs. cream cheese
3 eggs
3/4 C. sugar
2 tsp. vanilla

Combine graham crackers with butter and pat over the bottom and sides of a 9" pie pan. Bake in a 450°F. oven 4 minutes. Allow to cool.
Mix cream cheese, eggs, sugar and vanilla. Pour into crust and bake about 20 minutes at 350° F. or until set like custard. Allow to cool 5 minutes.

Topping:

1 C. commercial sour cream
3/4 tsp. sugar
1/4 tsp. almond extract

Spread topping and place cake back in oven about 5 minutes longer. Cool thoroughly before serving. Sprinkle lightly with cinnamon if desired. Serves 6-8.

PUMPKIN CHEESECAKE WITH BOURBON SOUR CREAM TOPPING

Pie Crust:

3/4 C. graham cracker crumbs
1/2 C. finely chopped pecans
1/4 C. light brown sugar, firmly packed
1/4 C. granulated sugar
1/2 stick unsalted butter, melted and cooled.

C ombine the cracker crumbs, pecans and sugars in a bowl or food processor. Stir in the butter. Press the mixture into the bottom and 1/2" up the side of a buttered 9" springform pan. Chill the crust for 1 hour.

Filling:

1$\frac{1}{2}$ C. solid pack pumpkin
3 large eggs
1$\frac{1}{2}$ tsp. cinnamon
$\frac{1}{2}$ tsp. freshly ground nutmeg
$\frac{1}{2}$ tsp ground ginger
$\frac{1}{2}$ tsp. salt
$\frac{1}{2}$ C. light brown sugar, firmly packed
3 8oz. pkgs. cream cheese, cut into bits and softened
$\frac{1}{2}$ C. granulated sugar
2 Tbs. heavy cream
1 Ts. corn starch
1 tsp. vanilla
1 Tb. bourbon liqueur or bourbon if desired

I n a bowl, whisk together the pumpkin, eggs, cinnamon, nutmeg, ginger, salt and brown sugar. In a large bowl, with an electric mixer cream together the cream cheese and granulated sugar; beat in the cream, cornstarch, vanilla, bourbon and the pumpkin mixture. Beat until smooth.

Pour the filling into the crust. Bake the cheesecake in the middle of a preheated 350° F. oven for 50 to 55 minutes, or until center is just set. Let it cool in the pan on a rack for 5 minutes.

Topping:

2 C. sour cream
2 Tbs. granulated sugar
1 Tbs. bourbon liqueur or bourbon, or to taste
16 pecan halves for garnish

I n a bowl, whisk together the sour cream, sugar and bourbon. Spread the mixture over the top of the cheesecake and bake the cheesecake for 5 minutes more. Let the cheesecake cool in the pan on a rack, then chill it, covered, overnight. Remove the side of the pan and garnish the top of the cheesecake with the pecans.

BLACK DOG CHEESECAKE

Pie Crust:

1 C. graham cracker crumbs (or vanilla wafers or hazelnuts)
Filling:
32 oz. cream cheese (room temperature)
1/2 C. whipping cream
1 3/4 C. sugar
4 eggs
1 tsp. vanilla

Mix filling ingredients until creamy. Butter the bottom and sides of a 9" springform pan. Line with the graham cracker crumbs and pour in filling mixture. Shake to level.

Put pan in another larger pan. Do not touch sides. Pour 1/2" boiling water around springform pan. (You can line the spring form pan with 2 layers of foil to prevent water seepage)

Place in a preheated 300°F. oven for 2 hours. Turn oven off and let sit for 1 hour. Remove and let sit on a rack for 2 hours before unmolding. Serves 6-8. *Black Dog Gallery, Longview, Texas*

NEVER-FAIL PIE CRUST

4 C. flour
2 C. shortening
1 Tb. sugar
1 1/2 tsps. salt
1 egg, beaten
1/2 C. water
1 Tb. vinegar

Mix flour, shortening, sugar and salt together using a fork until it reaches a crumbly consistency. Then mix egg, water and vinegar together and add to above mix. Do not use an electric mixer.

Version 2:
Go to the frozen foods department and buy Pet Pie Shells.

BANANA SPLIT PIE

Crust:

2 C. graham cracker crumb
1 stick margarine, melted

Mix well and press into 13" x 9" cake pan. Bake 15 minutes at 350° F.

Filling:

2 sticks softened margarine
2 eggs
2 C. powdered sugar
4 bananas
Small can of crushed pineapple
1-2 C. sliced strawberries
1/4 to 1/2 C. coconut
1 8oz. container of Cool Whip
Chopped nuts to sprinkle on top
Chocolate syrup to drizzle
Marachino cherries for garnish

Mix margarine with powdered sugar and add eggs. Beat on high speed until fluffly. Pour on top of cooled crust. Cut bananas lengthwise and then in quarters. Drizzle with lemon juice to prevent them from turning brown. Place on top of filling. Drain pineapple and sprinkle on top of bananas. Layer on strawberries, sprinkle cocoanut over all. Top with Cool Whip, then sprinkle on your favorite chopped nuts, drizzle with chocolate syrup, and garnish with cherries. Chill.

KEY LIME PIE

4 eggs, separated
3 oz. key lime juice
1 can sweetened condensed milk

Mix the egg yolks, lime juice and milk. Pour into a baked pie shell and top with meringue from the egg whites. Lightly brown mweringue.
The Cake Box, Marathon, Florida

CRAZY CRUST APPLE PIE

1 C. flour
1 tsp. baking powder
1/2 tsp. salt
2 Tbs. sugar
2/3 C. shortening
1 egg
3/4 C. water
1 can apple pie filling
1 Tbs. lemon juice
1/2 tsp. cinnamon

Sift the first four ingredients into a bowl. Add shortening, egg and water. Beat at low speed to blend, then beat 2 minutes at medium speed. Spoon into greased 10" pie pan. Combine remaining ingredients. Carefully spoon filling into center of batter. Do not stir. Bake 40 to 45 minutes or until crust is golden. Bake at 425° F.

LEMON MERINGUE PIE

1 can Eagle Brand milk
3 egg yolks
Juice of 3 lemons

Beat eggs and add milk. When well blended, add lemon juice. Pour into an unbaked pie shell and bake at 350°F. until done. Top with meringue and brown. Serve chilled.

EGG CUSTARD PIE

½ C. sugar
1½ C. milk
3 egg yolks
3 Tbs. flour
1 tsp. vanilla
3 egg whites
3 Tbs. sugar

Mix sugar and flour; beat egg yolks; add milk and vanilla and mix all together. Pour in unbaked pie shell and bake at 350°F. until done. Beat egg whites until stiff. Add the 3 Tbs. sugar and mix well. Spread on pie and return to oven until lightly browned.

CHERRY CREAM PIE

1 pkg. 8 oz. cream cheese
1 can Eagle Brand milk
⅓ C. lemon juice
1 can cherry pie filling or glaze

Cream cheese until fluffy, add milk and blend well. Add lemon juice and vanilla and mix well. Pour into a baked pie crust. Chill 2 to 3 hours, garnish top with cherry pie filling

For glaze instead of pie filling:

To ¾ C. cherry juice, add 3 Tbs. sugar, 3 Tbs. cornstarch, mix well and cook over low heat constantly until thick and clear. Remove from heat, stir in a few drops of red food coloring and 1 C. cherries. Allow to cool and spread on pie.

STRAWBERRY CREAM PIE

Pie Crust:

1 stick margarine (minus 1¹/₂ Tbs.)
1 C. flour
2 Tbs. powdered sugar

Melt the margarine and pour over the flour sifted with the powdered sugar. Pat into a 8" or 9" pie plate and bake at 325°F. for 25 minutes. Cool.

Filling:

2 C. milk
1 stick margarine
1 C. sugar
5 Tbs. flour

Heat the milk and the margarine until margarine is melted. Add the sugar, mixed well with the flour. Cook until fairly thick, stirring constantly. This may take 10 to 15 minutes. Remove from heat. Add 1 tsp. vanilla. Cool thoroughly.

Wash, hull and drain 1 pint of berries. Place whole (or halved, depending on the size) berries in bottom of cooled pie shell. Save some of the berries for garnish on top of pie. Spread crust with filling.

Whip 1 C. whipping cream and 5 Tbs. granulated sugar. Add ¹/₈ tsp. vanilla when cream is almost whipped stiff. Spread on top of filling. Place reserved berries on top of pie for decoration. Chill until ready to serve, at least 2 to 3 hours. This may also be made with fresh peaches or bananas.

COCONUT PINEAPPLE PIE

1 can angel flake coconut
1 small can crushed pineapple
2 sticks margarine
6 eggs
2 heaping Tbs. flour
2 C. sugar
1 C. white Karo syrup

ix the ingredients and place mixture in an unbaked pie crust. Cook in a 400° F. oven until done. Cool and top with whipped cream. Makes 2 pies.

CHOCOLATE PIE

1½ C. sugar
1½ C. milk
3 Tbs. flour or corn starch
3 egg yolks
3 Tbs. Hershey's cocoa
1 tsp. vanilla

Mix sugar, cocoa and flour. Beat egg yolks, add milk and vanilla; mix all together and pour into an unbaked pie shell. Bake at 350° F. until done. Beat egg whites stiff, then add 3 Tbs. sugar, mix and put on pie. Place in oven to brown. (Pie filling may be cooked in a double broiler and then put into a baked pie shell).

PINEAPPLE PIE

3 egg yolks
1 C. sugar
2 Tbs. flour
1 C. milk
1 tsp. vanilla
1 can crushed pineapple

Mix all ingredients together. Pour into an unbaked pie crust and bake in a 400° F. oven until done. Beat egg whites stiff and put on top of filling, then brown.

GREAT GRANDMOTHER'S PUMPKIN PIE

1 29 oz. can pumpkin puree
1 qt. whole milk
1½ C. brown sugar
½ C. maple syrup
4 egg whites, beaten
4 egg yolks, beaten
½ tsp. salt
1 tsp. cinnamon
1 tsp. ginger
Tart plum jam
Whipped cream

Place pumpkin in a large bowl. In a separate bowl, mix salt and spices with the sugar. Add to pumpkin. Fold in syrup, egg whites, egg yolks and milk. Bake in 2 unbaked pie shells in a 375° F. oven for 1 hour. When cold, spread with plum jam. Serve with whipped cream. Makes 2 pies.

AUNT NORINE'S CONCORD GRAPE PIE

4 C. Concord grapes
1 C. sugar
¼ C. all-purpose flour
¼ tsp. salt
1 Tb. lemon juice
1½ Tbs. butter, melted
1 9-inch unbaked pastry shell

Slip skins from grapes. Set skins aside. Bring pulp to a boil, reduce heat and simmer 5 minutes. Press through a sieve and remove seeds. Combine sugar, flour and salt. Add lemon juice, butter and grape pulp.

Into a pastry lined pie plate, add skins. Pour sugar mixture into pie plate. Lattice top with pastry strips, and sprinkle with cinnamon. Bake in a 350°F. oven 45 minutes, or at 450° F. for 15 minutes.

-

BANANA CREAM PIE

2/3 C. sugar
1/2 C. all-purpose flour
1/2 tsp. salt
2 C. milk
3 egg yolks, slightly beaten (save the whites for meringue)
2 Tb. butter
2 tsp. vanilla
2 bananas thinly sliced

In the top of a double boiler, combine sugar, flour and salt, stir in milk and cook, stirrring, over boiling water until mixture thickens, about 10 minutes.

Pour half the hot mixture into the beaten eggs, stirring until smooth. Return eggs to the rest of the hot mixture, and continue cooking until thickened.

Remove from heat, stir in vanilla and butter and allow to cool slightly. Place bananas in a baked pie shell and cover with the cream filling. Top with meringue and brown lightly.

JACKS MARVELOUS BROWNIES

2/3 C. butter
2 C. sugar
3 eggs
1 C. flour
1/4 tsp. salt
2 oz. unsweetened chocolate, melted
1 Tb. vanilla
1 C. chopped pecans

Cream butter and sugar. Beat in eggs just until blended. Sift flour and salt; stir gradually into egg mixture. Blend in melted chocolate and vanilla; add pecans. Spread in well greased 9" x 13" pan and bake ar 350° F. degrees for about 25 minutes. Cut into 1 1/2" squares when cool. Serve with whipped cream or vanilla ice cream. Makes 48 brownies.

BUFFALO CHIPS

2 C. margarine
4 eggs, well-beaten
4 C. flour
1 C. pecans, chopped
2 C. uncooked oatmeal
3 C. corn flakes
1 C. coconut
2 C. brown sugar
2 C. white sugar
2 tsps. baking powder
2 tsps. baking soda
2 tsps vanilla
6 oz. pkg. semisweet chocolate chips
6 oz. pkg. milk chocolate chips
6 oz. pkg. butterscotch chips

Mix all ingredients well. Chill in refrigerator 2 hours. Drop by table spoons on cookie sheet. Bake at 350° F. for 10-12 minutes. Serves an army.

THE FAMOUS $250 COOKIE RECIPE

We've heard several versions of this story, about an innocent party tasting a cookie, (sometimes the story says she was in Neiman-Marcus, sometimes it has to do with a Mrs. Fields outlet, sometimes it has been told to happen in other well-known restaurants, but it all has the same ending...) and asking for the recipe. When told there would be a charge of two-fifty, the party agreed, and later got a bill for $250! No mistake...So here's that famous $250 recipe!

2 C. butter
2 C. sugar
2 C. brown sugar
4 eggs
2 tsps. vanilla
4 C. flour
5 C. blended oatmeal (Measure and blend in a blender to a fine powder.)

1 tsp. salt
2 tsps. baking powder
2 tsps. baking soda
24 oz. chocolate chips
1 8-oz. grated Hershey candy bar
3 C. chopped nuts

Cream butter and both sugars. Add eggs and vanilla. Mix together with flour, oatmeal, salt, baking powder, and baking soda. Add chips, candy, and nuts. Roll into balls and place 2 inches apart on cookie sheet. Bake for 6 minutes at 375° F. Makes 112 cookies. Recipe may be halved.

DR. DOG'S FAVORITE COOKIES

3¹/₂ C. all-purpose flour
2 C. whole wheat flour
1 C. rye flour
1 C. corn meal
2 C. cracked wheat
¹/₂ C. dry milk
4 tsp. salt
1¹/₄ oz. pkg. active dry yeast
¹/₄ C. warm water
1 pint chicken stock
1 egg
1 Tb. milk

Preheat oven to 300° F. In a large bowl, combine flours, corn meal, cracked wheat, dry milk and salt. Combine yeast and water, add to dry ingredients along with stock. Beat egg and milk. Add to other ingredients.

Turn mixture onto a floured surface and knead for three minutes. Dough will be very stiff. Roll out to a ¹/₄" thickness. Cut dough with cookie cutters. (Dr. Dog is partial to little Christmas trees.) Bake on ungreased cookie sheets for 45 miutes. Turn off heat and dry cookies in over overnight. Store in an airtight container, clearly labeled "Dog Cookies."

PUP-POURRI

HERBS, SAUCES, & SEASONINGS

ROUX (PRONOUNCED "ROO")

Roux is an equal mixture of oil and flour that is browned and used as a thickening base for many south Louisiana dishes, such as gumbos and etouffees. In pre-microwave days, making a roux meant standing by the stove, stirring the flour and oil almost constantly so it would brown but not burn. Now, use the microwave for quick, easy and tasty roux.

2/3 C. oil
2/3 C. flour
2 C. onion, chopped
1 C. celery, chopped
1/2 C. green bell pepper, chopped
4 cloves garlic, minced
1/4 C. parsley, chopped
1/4 C. green onion tops, chopped
Approx. 1/4 C. hot water

Mix oil and flour together in a 4-cup measure. Microwave uncovered on high 6-7 minutes. Stir at 6 minutes. Roux will be light brown at this time and will need to cook 30 seconds to 1 minute to reach the desired dark brown color. The roux will be very hot, so use caution when touching the cup or bowl used in this process.

Add onion, celery, and bell pepper to roux. Stir and return to microwave. Saute on high 3 minutes. Add garlic, parsley, and green onion to roux, stir and return to microwave. Saute on high 2 minutes.

You should have about 3 3/4 C. of roux now. If any oil has risen to the top, pour it off. Slowly add enough hot tap water to bring roux to the 4-cup mark. Stir and you will have a smooth, dark roux in only 12 minutes. Roux freezes well.

CAROL'S RED PEPPER SATAY SAUCE

A satay is a Thai dish consisting of skewered strips of marinated chicken or beef on pre-soaked bamboo skewers, grilled and served with this sauce, rice, and a cucumber garnish.

2 pimientos (or 2 red bell peppers, or 1 jar pimientos)
1 small onion, chopped
2 large cloves garlic, chopped
2 Tbs. peanut oil
4 tsps. curry paste
2 tsps. Key West lime juice
1 tsp. fresh ground ginger
1 can (slightly over 1 C. cream of coconut
1/2 C. creamy peanut butter
1 tsp. sugar

Saute onions and garlic in peanut oil. Halve pimientos and broil, skin side up, until skin blackens and shrivels. Hold pimientos under cold water and remove skins, seeds, and veins. Add curry paste and ginger to oil mixture. Chop pimientos and add to oil mixture. Add lime juice. Simmer. In a separate saucepan, bring coconut cream to a boil. Add pimiento mixture to coconut cream. Add peanut butter and sugar. Simmer until well blended. Pour sauce into blender and puree. Return to saucepan and simmer until ready to use. Can be refrigerated overnight and reheated. Serves 3-4.

Suggested marinades for skewered meat:

Chicken:	Beef
Peanut oil	Peanut oil
Soy sauce	Soy sauce
1/2 lime, squeezed	Clove garlic
Fresh cilantro	Curry powder
Clove garlic	Cumin
Cumin	Turmeric
Turmeric	Coriander
	Ginger
	Red pepper

HOMEMADE BAR-B-QUE SAUCE

1 8 oz. can tomato paste
2 8 oz. cans of tomato sauce
1 C. vinegar
4 Tbs. Worcestershire sauce
2 C. water
1½ tsp. black pepper
½ C. chopped onion
Salt

Combine all ingredients, mix and simmer for 15 minutes.

Basting sauce:
½ C. vinegar
1 C. sauce (above)
4 C. water
2 Tbs. salt
2 Tbs. black pepper
Mix and use to baste meat as it slow-cooks on the grill.

BASIL PRESERVED IN OIL

4 C. unblemished fresh basil leaves, rinsed thoroughly and dried
½ C. olive oil plus extra to top off container

Place 1 C. basil and ½ C. oil in blender. Process until the leaves are chopped into fine pieces. Do not puree. Add the remaining leaves in 1-cup batches, blending until incorporated before adding the next batch.

Scrape the mixture into a noncorrodible container and pour enough oil on top to cover by 1 inch. Cover container and store at room temperature. To use preserved basil in recipes that call for fresh basil, simply dip out the appropriate amount and strain the oil back into the container. After using the basil oil, replaced with enough fresh oil to cover by at least 1 inch. The fresh oil will take on the basil's aroma in a week. If the leaves are scrupulously dried and the oil is conscientiously replaced after each use, the preserved basil will keep for 4-6 months.

MAYONNAISE AND VARIATIONS

Quick and Easy Mayonnaise:
1 large egg
5 tsp. fresh lemon juice
1 tsp. Dijon-style mustard
1/4 tsp salt
1/4 tsp. white pepper
1 C. vegetable oil, olive oil, or combination of both

In a blender with the motor on high, or in a food processor, blend the egg, lemon juice, mustard, salt and white pepper. Add the oil in a slow stream. Makes about 1 C.

Chipotle Mayonnaise
Same as above, adding 1/4 C. drained canned chipotle peppers in adobo sauce, available at Mexican markets and gourmet sections of larger supermarkets. Makes about 1 1/4 C.

Light Curry Mayonnaise:
Same as above, adding 1 tsp. curry powder or to taste. When mayonnaise is thickened in blender, transfer to a bowl and stir in 1/3 C. plain yogurt. Makes about 1 1/3 C.

Tarragon Aioli
To 1 1/4 C. mayonnaise add 1-2 Tbs. minced garlic, 2 Tbs. minced fresh tarragon leaves, 1 tsp. grated lemon peel, 3 Tbs. lemon juice, and 1 tsp. Dijon mustard, and salt to taste. Mix well. Divine on roasted potatoes or roast or rack of lamb.

THE HOLLANDAISE FAMILY

The Hollandaise sauce "family" consists of hollandaise, bearnaise, maltaise, choron, sabayon, etc., all variations a on a delicious theme.

Bearnaise is made with wine, vinegar, shallots and tarragon instead of the lemon juice of hollandaise.

Maltaise is orange flavored Hollandaise.

Choron is tomato flavored bearnaise.

Sabayon is Hollandaise with cream and a white wine fish stock.

You can make up your own.

BASIC HOLLANDAISE, MADE IN A BLENDER

1 stick butter, melted
3 egg yolks
Salt and white pepper to taste
A dash of Tabasco or a pinch of cayenne (optional)
1 or 2 Tb. lemon juice (to taste)

Place all ingredients except butter in a blender jar, and blend briefly. Withthe blender still running, slowly pour the melted butter into the jar and blend until smooth.

CHIPOTLENAISE

3 egg yolks
1 stick butter, melted
2 Tbs. chipotle hot sauce

In a blender, combine the chipotle hot sauce and three egg yolks. Blend briefly, then add the melted butter in a slow steady stream and blend until thickened.

BEARNAISE SAUCE

3 egg yolks
1 stick butter, melted
1/4 C. wine vinegar
1/4 C.dry white wine or vermouth

1 Tb.minced green onion
1/2 Tb.dried tarragon
Salt and pepper

Combine the wine, vinegar, onion, tarragon and salt and pepper to taste and microwave or boil until reduced to 2 tablespoons.

In a blender, combine the wine, vinegar mixture and three egg yolks. Blend briefly, then add the melted butter in a slow steady stream and blend until thickened.

BASIL HOLLANDAISE

3 egg yolks
1 stick butter, melted
2 Tbs. lemon juice
1 Tb. olive anchovy paste
1/2 C. minced fresh basil
Salt and pepper to taste

In a blender, combine the lemon juice, olive anchovy paste, basil and three egg yolks. Blend briefly, then add the melted butter in a slow steady stream and blend until thickened.

ORANGE RUM HOLLANDAISE

3 egg yolks
1 stick butter, melted
1/4 Tb. triple sec
1 1/4 Tb. Myers rum
1 Tb. orange juice
2 tsp. grated orange zest

In a blender, combine the triple sec, rum, orange juice, orange zest and three egg yolks. Blend briefly, then add the melted butter in a slow steady stream and blend until thickened.

FETA CHEESE DRESSING

1/2 lb. Feta cheese, crumbled
2 C. mayonnaise
2 cloves garlic, minced
1/2 C. red wine vinegar
1 tsp. salad herb blend:

(4 tsp. each marjoram, basil, tarragon, parsley, chervil, celery salt,
chives. 1 tsp. each lemon thyme, summer savory, rosemary,
crumbled oregano.)
1 Tb. Worcestershire sauce
2 Tbs. olive oil

B lend together for a real "gee-whiz" dressing for salads, seafood,
chicken, and more.

SALSA MEXICANA

Fresh Mexican Sauce

1 medium tomato
4 Tbs. finely chopped white onion
2 Tbs. roughly chopped fresh cilantro
3 chiles serranos, finely chopped, with seeds
1/2 tsp. salt, or to taste
1/3 C. cold water

C hop the unskinned tomato and mix with the rest of the
ingredients. Although this can be made up to 3 hours ahead, it is best
made at almost the last minute, for it soon loses its crispness and the
cilantro its sharp flavor.

CARIBBEAN SALSA

2 C. mango, peeled and cut into 1/4 inch cubes
1/2 C. cucumber, peeled, seeded and cut into 1/4 cubes
1/4 C. fresh cilantro, chopped
2 Tbs. green onion, finely chopped
1/2 jalapeno pepper, seeded and finely chopped
3 Tbs. fresh lime juice
1 1/2 tsps. brown sugar
1 tsp. fresh ground ginger root, peeled and minced
Dash pepper

In medium-sized bowl combine mango, cucumber, cilantro, green onion, jalapeno, lime juice, brown sugar, ginger and pepper. Cover and refrigerate at least 1 hour to allow flavors to blend.

RED HOT PEPPER CHUTNEY

1 green pepper, cored and seeded
1 red pepper, cored and seeded
4 fresh jalapeno peppers
3/4 C. white wine vinegar
1/2 C. granulated sugar
1/2 C. (packed) brown sugar
1/2 C. crystallized ginger, slivered
1/2 C. golden raisins
2 cloves garlic, minced

Cut each bell pepper into 8 long strips, cut crosswise into 1/4 inch slices. Remove stems from the jalapenos and cut in half lengthwise Cut them into 1/4 inch slices with seeds.
　　　Stir the peppers and all remaining ingredients together in a 4 quart microwave safe casserole. Cook, uncovered, at full power (650-700 watts) until thick, 20 minutes. This keeps for 2 weeks, covered in the refrigerator. Makes 2 1/2 C.

GARLICKY CRANBERRY CHUTNEY

1 inch cube of fresh ginger, peeled
3 cloves garlic peeled and very finely chopped
1/2 C. apple cider or distilled white vinegar
4 Tbs. sugar
1/8 tsp. cayenne pepper
1 lb. can or jar of jellied cranberry sauce
1/2 tsp. salt
Freshly ground black pepper

Cut ginger into paper-thin slices. Stack the slices together and cut them into very thin slivers.

Combine the ginger slivers, garlic, vinegar, sugar and cayenne in a small pot. Simmer on medium for about 15 minutes or until there are about 4 Tbs. of liquid left (excluding the solids.) Add the cranberry sauce, salt and pepper. Mix and bring to a simmer. It will be a bit lumpy, but that is fine. Simmer on a gentle heat for about 10 minutes. Cool. Put in a jar and refrigerate. This will keep for several days. *Madhur Jaffrey's Cookbook*

FRESH CORIANDER CHUTNEY

1/2 tsp. cumin seeds
3 C. coriander sprigs, chopped
1/2 C. fresh mint leaves, chopped
1 small green Thai chile, minced
1 garlic clove, minced
2 Tbs. fresh lime juice
1/4 tsp. salt
1/2 tsp. freshly ground black pepper

In a small dry skillet, toast the cumin seeds over high heat until fragrant, about 30 seconds. Transfer the cumin to a mortar and pound to a coarse powder. Alternatively, chop the seeds finely with a knife.

In a food processor, combine the cumin with all the remaining ingredients. Process to a paste, stopping to scrape down the sides of the bowl once or twice. Scrape the chutney into a bowl and press plastic wrap directly on the surface. Refrigerate for up to 1 day. Makes about 1/2 C.

CUCUMBER RAITA

1 tsp. cumin seeds
1½ tsp. coriander seeds
1½ C. plain yogurt
Pinch of cayenne pepper
1 Tb. finely chopped onion
½ tsp. salt
½ tsp. freshly ground black pepper
1 large cucumber, peeled, halved lengthwise and thinly sliced

In a small dry skillet, toast the cumin and coriander seeds over high heat until fragrant, about 1 minute. Transfer the seeds to a mortar or spice mill and grind to a powder.

In a medium bowl, combine the ground cumin and coriander wtih all the remaining ingredients and stir well. Refrigerate for 1 hour to blend the flavors. Makes 6 servings.

An excellent condiment to accompany Indian-style dishes or anything hot that can use a "cool down".

GARAM MASALA

1 Tb. cardamom seeds
1 cinnamon stick
⅓ of a whole nutmeg
1 tsp. whole black peppercorns
1 tsp. black or regular cumin seeds
1 tsp. whole cloves

Put all the ingredients in a clean coffee grinder or spice mill and grind finely. Store in a lidded jar in a dark place. Makes 3 Tbs.

CURRY POWDER

Curry is not a substance in itself; it is actually a combination of spices.

2 tsps. coriander seeds
1/2 tsp. cumin seeds
2 cardamom pods, cut in half
2 whole cloves
1/2 tsp. ground mace
1/4 tsp. ground allspice
1 bay leaf, cut up very fine
3 thyme sprigs
1 tsp. fenugreek seeds
2 tsps. ground turmeric
2 small dried hot chili peppers

Grind these ingredients together in blender at high speed for at least 5 minutes, or with mortar and pestle until powdery.

TONY'S CAJUN SEASONING

1 26 oz. box salt
1 1/2 oz. ground black pepper
2 oz. ground red pepper
1 oz. pure garlic powder
1 oz. chili powder
1 oz. MSG

Mix thoroughly. Store in air tight container.
Tony Chachere's Cook Book

WEST INDIAN SEASONING

In the West Indies, long before commercial seasonings were available, people made up their own combinations of herbs and seasonings. They mixed them with salt and kept them to flavor meats, fish, soups or whatever...

$1/2$ C. salt
2 cut up cloves garlic
$1/2$ cut up medium onion
1 stalk celery with leaves
1 sprig parsley
2 tsps. ground black pepper
$1/4$ tsp. cloves
$1/2$ tsp. nutmeg
$1/4$ tsp. thyme

Grind all together until well mixed and moist. It will keep indefinitely in a jar on a shelf.
Dee Carstarphen, Maverick Sea Fare

DR. DOG'S SELECTED READING

COOKBOOKS

There are so many cookbooks and I have a lot of them, and I'm sure you are familiar with many on this list. These particular cookbooks are important for specific reasons which I have noted. I think readers of <u>Cooking with Dr. Dog</u> will find these of particular interest.

Carstarphen, Dee, <u>Maverick Sea Fare</u>, Pen and Ink Press, 1982
    This book gives the reader a wonderful "visit" aboard the charter vessel *Maverick*. The book is, happily, still available,

Child, Julia, <u>Julia Child & Company</u>, Alfred Knopf, 1978.
    Out-of-print, but you can find used copies fairly easily. These two volumes were based on Julia's TV series and are menu oriented.

Child, Julia, <u>Julia Child & More Company</u>, Alfred Knopf, 1979.
    Out-of-print

Child, Julia and Simone Beck, <u>Mastering the Art of French Cooking</u>, Volume I, Alfred Knopf, 1961, Volume II, Alfred Knopf, 1970.
    These marvelous books are available in several editions. If I could own only two cookbooks, these would be the two.

Child, Julia, <u>From Julia's Kitchen</u>, Alfred Knopf, 1975.
    All of Julia Child's books are filled with information and <u>exact</u> instructions on how to make things work. Anyone who can read and follow directions <u>can </u>master the art of French cooking. Back in print as of October 1999!

Child, Julia, <u>The Way to Cook</u>, Alfred Knopf, 1989
    A comprehensive volume covering just about everything.

Cunkle, James and Carol, <u>Kokopelli's Cook Book,</u> Golden West Publishers, 1997.

The authors of this book have been involved with the Raven Site Ruin at White Mountain Archaeolgical Center near St. Johns, Arizona for more than a decade. The cook book offers an interesting insight into the foods and cooking methods of the American Southwest. You can order Kokopelli's Cook Book from Golden West Publishers, 4113 N. Longview Ave., Phoenix, AZ 85014. For a free catalog of all their publications, call 1-800-658-5830

Gunst, Kathy, Roasting, Macmillan 1995,
One of the most fun cook books I have picked up in a while. How to roast everything! Keeps you out of the kitchen a lot in those hot summer months. Not currently available.

Hawkes, Alex D., The Flavors of the Caribbean and Latin America, Viking Press, 1978
Alex Hawke's recipes collected during his career as a botanist in the Caribbean and Latin America are different, exciting, and an immersion in the cultures of South America. Long out of print ,I found a few copies on the internet through www. bibliofind.com. A little expensive, but worth it.

Hinchman, Melissa Davis, Editor, True Grits, Junior League of Atlanta, 1995.
The Atlanta Junior League's True Grits, published in the fall of 1995, is one of the most refreshing and useable cookbooks I've read in a long time.

Hooper, Lisa A., Editor, The Healthy Heart Cookbook, Oxmoor Press, 1992.
This book gives you low-fat, heart-healthy food, done really well.

Jaffrey, Madhur, Madhur Jaffrey's Indian Cooking, Barron's, 1982.
If you like Indian cuisine and you want to learn to do it practically and with items generally available in the U.S., then this is the book that will show you how. An expanded edition, published in 1995 is available.

Jaffrey, Madhur, Madhur Jaffrey's Cookbook, Harper & Row, 1989.
Madhur Jaffrey's Cookbook is a wonderful fusion of East and West and covers the gamut from Ecuadoran pork roast to San Antonio huevos rancheros to Thai noodle soup. Unfortunately, it is out-of-print.

Kennedy, Diana, The Cuisines of Mexico, Harper & Row, 1988.

Diana Kennedy is the "high priestess" of Mexican cooking. Her book is well-written and explained. If you like the food of Mexico, you can spend many happy hours here. Available in paperback.

Prudhomme, Paul, Chef Paul Prudhomme's Louisiana Kitchen, William Morrow, 1984.

K-Paul's Restaurant in New Orleans started the Cajun rage, and the chef's book is a good place to start learning what it's all about. It is available.

Robinson, Jan, Ship to Shore, 1983; Ship to Shore II, 1986, and Sip to Shore, 1986, privately published, Charlotte, NC.

Jan, a charter boat captain herself, has collected the recipes for food and drink from all the famous charter yachts in the Caribbean. Great recipes and full of short cuts to preparing great food. Write to Ship to Shore,10500 Mount Holly Rd, Charlotte, NC 28214

Rombauer, Irma S. and Marion Rombauer, The Joy of Cooking, Bobbs-Merrill, 1975.

A must-have encyclopedia of information and recipes for just about anything you could ever want to know about food and food preparation. A new version has recently been released.

Rosso, Julee and Sheila Lukins, The Silver Palate Cookbook, Workman, 1982.

This book offers some good food and some original ideas.

Sheraton, Mimi, The Seducer's Cookbook, Random House, 1963.

Mimi Sheraton's book, published 36 years ago, is still a hoot, offering sage advice on the fine art of the gastronomic approach to seduction. Out of print.

Sunset Cookbooks. Sunset publishes many cookbooks on different cuisines. They are sensible, easy to do and very good. I'm not certain of availability. The Italian book shows to be out of print.

MAGAZINES

Eating Well--Alas, my all-time favorite cooking magazine ceased publication in Spring 1999. Healthy but not fanatically so, this magazine published wonderful articles and wonderful recipes. There are several collections of favorite recipes from the magazine.

Food and Wine--Jill eagerly awaits the monthly appearance of F&W, because she knows something new, different and exciting will be on the table that night as I explore the many creative recipes and menus in each issue.

Sunset-- A magazine for and about the West Coast, it offers exciting stories and recipes from The western United States and Canada.

INTERNET RESOURCES

For new and out of print books, try www.amazon.com

For the really hard to find books, my best luck has been with www.bibliofind.com It is a network of bookstores all over the country.

INDEX

ORDER **COOKING WITH DR. DOG** AND DR. DOG ACCESSORIES FOR YOURSELF AND FRIENDS

Cooking with Dr. Dog	$16.95
Cooking with Dr. Dog Aprons	$10.95
Cooking with Dr. Dog Grocery Bags	$10.95
Cooking with Dr. Dog T-Shirts	$12.95

Please send me _____ Copies of **Cooking with Dr. Dog** @ $16.95 each = _____

Please send me _____ Cooking with **Dr. Dog Aprons** @ $10.95 each = _____

Please send me _____ Cooking with **Dr. Dog Grocery Bags** @ $10.95 each = _____

Please send me _____ Cooking with **Dr. Dog T-shirts** @ $ 12.95 each = _____

SUBTOTAL _____

North Carolina residents add 6% state sales tax   TAX _____

TOTAL _____

SHIPPING AND HANDLING INCLUDED

Ship to_____ Address _____

City_____ State_____ Zip_____

Credit Card Info: MC VISA Number_____Exp. date_____

Make checks payable to Jerry Jones

Mail to: Jerry Jones, 102 Connally St., Black Mountain, NC 28711

Phone and Fax 828-669-1600

Visit us on-line at http://www.mindspring.com/~dr dog

or email your questions and comments to: drdog@mindspring.com